Elli Samuels' passion for cooking and sharing shines through this volume like light through glass. Her guided approach is aimed at food enthusiasts with varied cooking abilities, from complete beginners on up. If you care about healthy eating, but wouldn't think of sacrificing deliciousness, this book is in the right hands! Many recipes are written as if Elli is in the kitchen with you. However, for even more direction, the Helping Hand section is your second guide. It's there to anticipate and answer questions you might have as you plan to make one of the dishes. With basic techniques and useful tips such as how to boil an egg, how to make strawberries last, and how to select and prepare kale, you're covered!

Ultimately, Elli has you and your cooking in mind. "To Your Health Quick Tips" begins with her basic philosophy for selecting and buying food, one that she hopes you'll adopt! "Kitchen Tools" lists all the kitchen tools you'll need to follow the recipes in the book, while "Elli's Pantry" lists building block pantry items you'll find handy to have around. The "Snack!" section points you to some healthy pick-me-ups, and when you want to put your home cooked meals together, Elli's menu suggestions will give you a head start. As venerated chef Julia Child once said,

"You don't have to cook fancy or complicated masterpieces - just good food from fresh ingredients."

Cooking with Elli will help you do just that!

Cooking *with* Elli

A DELICIOUS GUIDE FOR BUDDING FOODIES AND BEYOND

Elli Samuels

BOOK PUBLISHERS NETWORK

Changing the World One Book at a Time

Book Publishers Network
P.O. Box 2256
Bothell • WA • 98041
Ph • 425-483-3040
www.bookpublishersnetwork.com

10 9 8 7 6 5 4 3 2 1

Printed in the United States of America

LCCN 2013950662
ISBN 978-1-940598-07-9Book

Cover and Layout Design: Alyssa Renee Design

A delicious meal, no matter how small,
is the starting point for nurturing the body and soul.

- Quote in the window of a vibrant little restaurant in Cambridge, MA

DEDICATION:

I would like to dedicate this book to the love of my life, my husband, Tom, who has supported me in every way and at every turn. I am lucky that he loves food and doesn't mind how much I like to talk about it!

ACKNOWLEDGEMENTS:

I thank my children, Danielle and Benjy, with great love and enthusiasm since they and their friends were the inspiration for the concept of my book. They, too, appreciate good food, and I hope I have inspired them to revel in food possibilities and to create "keeper" dishes for their families one day. Special thanks to Danielle for the fun times we spent consulting about various aspects of the book.

I thank my mother for feeding me wonderful, over-the-top dishes from our family kitchen and for being a fit example from her days of running the track at my high school! I thank my father, of blessed memory, for being unquestionably my biggest fan in life. His appetite was one any cook would adore. Of course, he appreciated everything I made, including simple eggs for breakfast on days he would stop by in the morning after shul.

I thank my family, and my friends who are like family to me, for tasting and enjoying my food over the years. It has brought me incredible pleasure.

The photographs in this book were beautifully created by my husband's uncle, mitch samuels grystar, an accomplished artist who I am so lucky to have in my life; by Michelle Able, a wonderful photographer with a natural touch who I am privileged to have gotten to know; and by my daughter Danielle, who tapped into her creative side with such ease and energy. On the design side, I am so fortunate to have Alyssa Wible's talent grace these pages.

Finally, thank you ever so much, to each and every one of my recipe testers who took the time to respond, shop, cook, and respond again with their invaluable feedback, encouragement, and excitement. I could not have done it without you.

The best thing you can do so that you eat nutritiously is to learn how to cook.

- Author Unknown

TABLE OF CONTENTS

APPENDIX

RECIPE INDEX

Hi! My name is Elli Samuels. I wouldn't say that I am *all* about food, but I will admit that my passion for it is fairly unleashed. I love eating great food, talking about great food, creating new recipes, and talking about newly created recipes. Whose bedtime reading can be a joyous page-by-page exploration of a newly acquired cookbook or food magazine? That would be mine. I am in my element as I wander, at my meandering pace, through distinctive food shops. Whether it is a traditional Italian grocery store in Boston's North End, a specialty spice shop in Israel, or our favorite weekly farmer's market in Hood River, Oregon, I am happily amused. I love to jot down a few notes about a menu item or a dish that we enjoy during such travels, planning to make my own version at home. It's an "I could make that" mentality. Even better, I fully embrace the challenge of making a dish healthier and still delicious!

When I was growing up, Mom was the cook, and her reputation as a consummate one was well deserved. Dinner guests at our house could count on scrumptious Mediterranean entrees, sides, and salads galore. However, Mom left the baking to me. I added my touch with cakes, pies, and cookies made from scratch.

My culinary skills did take a little while to fully develop though. My husband would agree that I have come a long way from the early days of our marriage. Back then, our staple dinner was BBQ chicken (translates to chicken topped with some bottled barbecue sauce), rice, and canned green beans.

When I started writing this book, I had my then-college-age kids and their friends in mind. They liked my food, and I knew there was a wide range of cooking experience among them. I wanted to create a book that would benefit all levels. There was one of my son's friends (we'll call him Rex to protect the privacy of his rules!) who had a rule about his food preparation method – if it couldn't be cooked in a microwave, it was out! His second rule was about clean up. If dishwashing was required, forget it! There were also friends who wanted to go a little further to eat good food but had very little cooking experience. Then there were some like my daughter's friend, Kate, who would cook meals beyond most college kids' repertoire because she loved eating and creating nourishing, delicious food.

As I cooked and wrote, many recipes became what I consider a bit "food forward," celebrating flavor and ingredient combinations. While this book takes off from a "let's coach Rex" spot, I am confident that the Kate's out there will love the recipes as well.

Whatever your age, maybe you have very little experience, or could use a serious confidence boost in the kitchen. Or, perhaps you would like to add some great variety to your cooking adventures. I have written many recipes as though I am in the kitchen with you and I have tried to anticipate questions you might have along the way. In the interest of creativity and variety, I have utilized some foods that might be a little new to some, like root vegetables, fennel, okra, and kale. Budding and blossoming foodies, this book's for you!

The interest in local and organic food has been sweeping the country, and it's truly a rocking time in the world of cooking and eating. This fresh and healthy approach has inspired many of my recipes (well, there are a few indulgent desserts, but you just have to go for it sometimes!). While food isn't cheap these days, and organic, better quality food costs even more, your well-being is worth it.

SO, if you want to get started…
You don't need cooking experience or knowledge,
You don't need fancy equipment,
BUT you do need to enjoy tasty food.

I think you will find the following parts of the book really useful:

- A HELPING HAND walks you through basic techniques such as how to properly measure ingredients, the difference between mincing and dicing, how to separate an egg, and how to tell when fish is done. Also, you'll find help here when it comes to selecting and preparing certain fruits and veggies (Appendix 1).

- "TO YOUR HEALTH" QUICK TIPS which I hope will inspire your healthy and creative eating (Appendix 2).

- KITCHEN TOOLS you'll need to make the recipes in the book (Appendix 3).

- ELLI'S PANTRY of handy ingredient staples (Appendix 4).

- SNACK! ideas that pick you up tastily and healthfully (Appendix 5)

- SUGGESTED MENUS to streamline time spent pairing recipes for your meals (Appendix 6).

Browse the Helping Hand section and be on your way!

"When you wake up in the morning, Pooh," said Piglet at last, "what's the first thing you say to yourself?"

"What's for breakfast," said Pooh. "What do you say, Piglet?"

"I say, 'I wonder what's going to happen exciting today?'" said Piglet.

Pooh nodded thoughtfully.

"It's the same thing." he said.

- A. A. Milne, The House at Pooh Center

RISE + *shine*

Golden Apricot Scones

....

Yield: 16 mini scones.

Apricot scones have become part of our Samuels family Thanksgiving tradition, and our guests look forward to seeing freshly baked baskets of these little treats on the table every year! I must say, Thanksgiving morning simply wouldn't be the same without my flour-smudged daughter and me putting these scones together, while my husband and son eagerly await "testing" them as soon as they exit the oven!

2 c. plus 1 Tbsp. flour

¼ cup sugar

2 tsp. baking powder

½ tsp. baking soda

½ tsp. salt

1/3 cup cold butter, cut into small cubes

2/3 cup plain nonfat Greek yogurt, plus 2 Tbsp. skim milk

2/3 cup dried apricots, chopped

1 egg, beaten, for glaze

Brown sugar for sprinkling

Optional: If you would like to indulge in a richer, slightly more dense scone, substitute 2/3 cup sour cream for the Greek yogurt and milk.

Preheat the oven to 400 degrees.

Spray a cookie sheet with Pam, and have a small pastry brush handy.

Chop your apricots so they are ready to go. Mix the flour, sugar, baking powder, baking soda, and salt in large bowl. Add the butter and mix with your fingertips (you don't want to dawdle and let the butter become too soft) until crumbly. (For a visual: the butter pieces will be about pea sized and coated with flour.)

Mix the yogurt and milk in a small bowl. Make an indentation about the size of your fist in the middle of the flour mixture and add the yogurt. Mix with a fork, gradually incorporating the flour, until it starts to come together. Give the mixture a couple of squeezes with your hands in order to bring it together (most of the way) into dough.

Turn the mixture onto a lightly floured surface, and sprinkle the apricots on top. Knead (fold the dough over itself, first from one side, then the other, and push with the heel of your hands) until the apricots are distributed throughout and you have a dough. Use your body weight and get into the motion!

Divide the dough in half, and flatten each piece into about a 4" round. Slice each round into 8 equal-sized wedges.

Transfer the scones to the baking sheet, and use the pastry brush to lightly coat the tops with beaten egg (gives them a nice shine). Sprinkle each scone with a bit of brown sugar.

Bake until lightly golden on the bottom, and a little golden on top, about 9-11 minutes. Try not to over-bake!

Variation: Substitute crystallized ginger and dates (about 1/2 cup total) for the apricots.

Zucchini, Fig, and Coconut Muffins

Yield: 12 large muffins.

Zucchini keeps these muffins moist, and the chewy figs are a nice, sweet surprise. I took some over to a friend, and she loved them! Great with a cup of tea…

1 cup flour

1 cup whole wheat pastry flour

1 tsp. cinnamon

½ tsp. nutmeg

2 tsp. baking powder

½ tsp. baking soda

½ tsp. salt

2 cups grated zucchini (about 2 medium, just under 1 lb.)

¾ cup chopped and dried Mission figs

½ cup sweetened shredded coconut

2 eggs

½ cup honey

½ cup Canola oil

1 Tbsp. vanilla

Preheat the oven to 375 degrees.

Spray your muffin tin with Pam.

Grate your zucchini and chop your figs. Don't forget to cut off (and discard) the stems on top of the figs. Set aside.

In a large bowl, whisk the flours, cinnamon, nutmeg, baking powder, baking soda, and salt together. Stir in the zucchini, figs, and coconut until they are coated with the flour mixture. In a medium bowl, whisk the eggs, honey, oil, and vanilla until well combined. Stir the egg mixture into the flour mixture, just until all the ingredients are moistened. Spoon the batter into the prepared muffin tin.

Bake for 18 minutes, until a toothpick inserted in the center comes out without batter attached. Try not to over-bake.

Enjoy.

Ginger Walnut Muffins with a Vanilla Cinnamon Glaze

....

Yield: 12 large muffins.

I love ginger snaps, gingerbread men, and ginger bread. So, it was natural for me to want to work on a ginger muffin recipe. For other ginger fans out there, these muffins will satisfy! They have a deep flavor, with a nice vanilla hit. And they're easy to make!

2 cups whole wheat flour

1 cup all-purpose flour

2 tsp. baking soda

1 tsp. baking powder

3 tsp. ground ginger

1 ½ tsp. cinnamon

¼ tsp. ground cloves

½ tsp. nutmeg

1/4 tsp. pepper

½ tsp. salt

2 cups unsweetened applesauce

2/3 cup molasses

1/3 cup Canola oil

3 eggs

1 cup walnut pieces

For the glaze:

1 cup powdered sugar

2 Tbsp. milk

½ tsp. vanilla

½ tsp. cinnamon

Preheat the oven to 350 degrees.

Spray your muffin tin well with Pam (some on top of the pan too, so any muffin over-hang won't stick).

Put the flours, baking soda, baking powder, ginger, cinnamon, cloves, nutmeg, pepper, and salt in a medium bowl and stir to combine. Set aside. Put the applesauce, molasses, oil, and eggs in a large bowl and combine well with a whisk. Add the dry to the wet ingredients and stir (a wooden spoon is good) just until combined. Add the walnuts and stir just until combined.

Transfer the batter to your muffin tin - I like to pour slowly while guiding the batter into the cups with a spoon. Fill each muffin container completely. Bake for about 22 minutes, or until a toothpick inserted in the center comes out without batter attached. If you have one, set the tin on a metal rack to cool.

To make the glaze, combine all the ingredients in a small bowl and stir well until smooth. Drizzle over the muffins (or spread with a knife) after they have cooled.

Sprouted Whole Grain Cranberry Orange Muffins

....

Yield: 12 muffins.

This recipe began as an experiment, as many do, and my family loved them. The muffins have a hearty, almost nutty texture and a sweet-tooth-satisfying taste, while staying in the healthy category. Mission accomplished!

1 cup wheat cereal nuggets (I use Ezekiel brand sprouted whole grain cereal. You could also use Grape Nuts)

1 cup uncooked regular oats

¼ cup sugar

½ cup whole wheat pastry flour

½ tsp. baking soda

½ tsp. salt

2 eggs

½ cup fat free plain yogurt

¼ cup canola oil

1 tsp. orange rind, minced (just the orange part of the skin, not the white)

¼ cup good quality orange marmalade (I like Dalfour brand because it contains wholesome ingredients and lots of orange rind)

1 cup fresh cranberries (or ½ cup dried)

Preheat the oven to 375 degrees.

Spray a muffin tin with Pam.

Put the cereal, oats, sugar, flour, baking soda and salt in a medium bowl and stir. Set aside. Whisk the eggs, yogurt, and oil together in a large bowl until combined. Add the dry ingredients and stir just until moistened. Add the orange marmalade, orange rind and cranberries and stir gently until combined.

Spoon the mixture, as equally as you can, into the muffin tins. Bake for 15-16 minutes, or until golden.

You don't want to overcook these, but you want them done in the middle, so test with a toothpick. It should come out without batter attached.

"Little Secret" Blueberry Muffins

....

Yield: 12 muffins.

Almost every place that sells muffins has a blueberry variety. They are a classic, but usually high in fat and often lacking in the texture department. Not true for these "little secrets." They are moist, have a fresh depth of flavor, and are definitely healthier than most!

2 cups flour

2 tsp. baking powder

1/4 tsp. salt

4 Tbsp. butter, room temperature*

4 oz. jar baby food sweet potatoes (1/2 cup)

¼ cup unsweetened applesauce

1 cup sugar

2 large eggs

1 tsp. vanilla

½ cup milk (1% preferred, but skim works too)

2 ½ cups frozen blueberries (or fresh, if in season)

Optional: 1 ½ tsp. lemon zest –just the yellow part of the skin (lends a special bright flavor to the recipe!)

*Hint: Who, but restaurants, has room temp butter hanging around? Well, what I do when I haven't remembered to take butter out way in advance of making a recipe (which is almost always!) is put it on a paper towel (still in the wrapping) in the microwave for small second increments, starting with 12 (then 4), until it is soft, but not melting.

Preheat the oven to 375 degrees.

Spray your muffin tin with Pam.

In a small bowl, stir the flour, baking powder and salt together to combine. Set aside.

With your electric mixer, beat the butter, sweet potatoes, and applesauce together until combined. Start SLOWLY so it won't splatter all over. Add the sugar and beat until well blended. Add the eggs and vanilla and combine thoroughly. Add the flour mixture, ½ at a time, alternating with the milk. If you need to stop to push the dry into the mixed ingredients with a spatula, do so. Stir the berries in with a wooden spoon. Fill the muffin cups (I like to tilt the bowl and guide the batter into the cups with a spoon- or use an ice cream scoop). Bake for about 22 minutes, until golden, or until a toothpick inserted in the center comes out without batter attached. Try not to over-bake.

Variation: If you love cranberries, substitute 1 cup of fresh cranberries for a cup of the blueberries, and you'll have delicious **blueberry cranberry muffins** (my husband's favorite!).

Pumpkin Bread, Pure and Simple

....

Makes one loaf.

Most pumpkin breads, zucchini breads, and even banana breads have a lot more fat and sugar than most people think! Not true for this pumpkin bread, and it's still moist, delicious, and loaded with flavor. Plus, the pumpkin spice aroma in the kitchen is a sweet bonus. Note some uses for leftover pumpkin puree at the end of the recipe.

½ cup sugar

½ cup brown sugar

¼ cup, plus 2 Tbsp. Canola oil

¼ cup unsweetened applesauce

2 eggs

1 cup canned pureed pumpkin

1¾ cups flour

½ tsp. baking powder

1 tsp. baking soda

1 tsp. salt

½ tsp. each of cloves, nutmeg, ginger, cinnamon, and all-spice*

1/3 cup low fat milk (I use 1%; any will do)

Optional add-ins: chocolate chips, dried cranberries, pumpkin seeds, walnuts

*Note: In case you don't have all of those spices, I had a friend test this recipe using "pumpkin pie spice" (found in the spice section at the store) and she said it came out great.

Preheat the oven to 350 degrees.

Spray a standard size loaf pan with Pam.

Whisk the sugars, oil, applesauce, eggs and pumpkin together in a large bowl. Mix the flour, baking powder, baking soda, salt and spices together in a small bowl. Add the dry mix to the wet in 2 additions, stirring until combined. Add the milk, and stir until well combined. Pour into your prepared loaf pan and bake for 55 minutes. Take a peek after about 45 minutes, and if the bread looks like it's turning pretty brown, just lay a piece of foil over the top while it cooks the rest of the way. It's ready when a toothpick inserted in the center comes out without batter attached. Try not to over-bake.

Let the bread cool completely before wrapping leftovers.

Some of my ideas for using leftover pumpkin puree:

- Put some in your protein smoothie.

- Add some to your oatmeal, with some brown sugar, pumpkin pie spices, and raisins.

- Add some to plain yogurt, with a little maple syrup and cinnamon.

- *Try this coffee drink:* 1 cup low fat milk, ½ cup water, heaping tsp. instant coffee, ½ tsp. vanilla, ¾ tsp. sugar, ½ tsp. cinnamon, pinch of nutmeg, heaping spoon of pumpkin (can just use just a soup spoon from your flatware set). Stir, and heat the mixture in a small saucepan over medium heat 'til steaming.

- Give some to your dog or cat! It's got great fiber and vitamins for pets.

To Your Health Crust-less Quiche

Serves 6.

There are so many possibilities for quiche; it's fun to be creative. The greens, sundried tomatoes, and cheese are the perfect backdrop for the winning flavor of this version. It may be low in fat, but not in taste! It's great for brunch, and leftovers make a quick and easy breakfast or snack.

10 oz. package of frozen chopped spinach, thawed and squeezed dry (can see method in "Warm Spinach Artichoke Dip" recipe)

10 oz. package of frozen collard greens OR (if you can't find that size) about ½ of a 16 oz. package, thawed and squeezed dry

¼ cup sundried tomatoes, chopped (the moist variety; not the ones packed in oil)

1/3 cup low-moisture part-skim grated mozzarella cheese

2 eggs

1 cup 2% cottage cheese

¼ cup nonfat plain yogurt

¼ tsp. garlic powder

¼ tsp. salt

¼ tsp. pepper

1/4 cup plus 1 Tbsp. grated parmesan cheese for sprinkling

Optional: Serve with sliced avocado and salsa on the side.

Preheat the oven to 350 degrees.

Spray a 9 inch glass pie plate with Pam.

Crumble the thawed and squeezed spinach and collard greens into a medium bowl (this makes it easier to mix in the remaining ingredients). Add the sundried tomatoes and the mozzarella cheese. Stir to combine and spread into the pie plate. Set aside.

In the same bowl, combine the eggs, cottage cheese, yogurt, garlic powder, salt, pepper, and ¼ cup parmesan cheese. Stir with a whisk until smooth. Pour over the vegetables. Sprinkle with 1 Tbsp. parmesan cheese. Bake for about 30 minutes or until the middle of the quiche is set (not jiggly).

Dad's "Special Eggs"

....

Serves 1- 2.

My Dad was famous for what he called "Special Eggs." I can still see him maneuvering around the kitchen, cranking these out for us kids. Eggs and toast, yes, but these are more fun to make and to eat!

Have a large skillet ready to use.

2 slices of bread (white or wheat)

1 ½ Tbsp. butter, softened (either leave out for a bit or microwave for a few seconds), divided

A juice size or small glass (or a biscuit cutter, if you happen to have one)

2 eggs

Pinch of salt and pepper to taste

Jam for circle toasts (optional)

Cut out a circle in the middle of each slice of bread with a biscuit cutter or by pressing down with an upside down juice glass (if you don't have a small glass or a biscuit cutter, you could just do your best at cutting a circle out). With about half of the butter, butter one side of each slice of bread and the bread circles. Set the circles aside.

Melt the remaining butter in your skillet over medium heat, and swirl it around so the bottom of the pan is coated. Put the bread slices in the pan, buttered side up, and crack an egg into each hole. It is safest to crack the egg into a measuring cup first to make sure you get no shell pieces, and then pour the egg into the hole.

Sprinkle with a bit of salt and pepper.

When the bread is golden on the bottom side (take a peak after about 3 minutes), flip them. At this point, add the circles to the pan, buttered side down and cook until toasted. When the bread is lightly toasted on the other side, they are done. Slide the "special eggs" onto a plate, spread the circles with some jam if you like, and enjoy!

Perfect, Simple Scrambled Eggs

....

Serves 2.

*It's really nice to be able to make great scrambled eggs --
moist and satisfying, customized to your liking! My father-in-
law says these are the best ever.*

½ Tbsp. butter

4 eggs

Pinch Kosher salt

Sprinkle of pepper, optional

Heat a large skillet over medium heat. In a small mixing bowl, whisk eggs pretty vigorously - you want to add some air for fluffiness.

Melt the butter over medium heat until it bubbles. Stir a pinch of Kosher salt (and pepper if desired) into egg mixture, then pour into pan. Immediately reduce the heat to medium-low. Don't stir the eggs right away-give them a chance to set a bit. Note that if you plan to add any ingredients (e.g. veggies, cheese), this is a good time to do it. With a wooden spoon, start to scrape the eggs from the edges to the center. Continue to scrape the spoon to move the eggs around as they cook. When the eggs are scrambled and look wet, but no longer liquid, remove from the heat and serve.

KEY: if they look done in the pan, they'll be over-done on the plate.

Cinnamon Brown Sugar
Quinoa Pudding with Toasted Almonds

Serves 6.

I was going to make rice pudding, but didn't really want to use white rice. I thought about brown rice. But then I thought quinoa would be the perfect choice- it is a complete protein and I love the texture. Well, I came up with this recipe that incorporates the traditional warm flavors of cinnamon and brown sugar. It is a fantastic recipe to make the night before. In the morning, you'll have a delicious, sustaining breakfast at your fingertips!

1 cup quinoa

3 1/2 cups 1% milk

2 eggs

1/3 cup raisins

3 ½ Tbsp. brown sugar

¼ tsp. cinnamon

1/8 tsp. nutmeg

1/8 tsp. salt

¼ cup sliced almonds, toasted

Bring the quinoa and 2 cups milk to a boil in a large (3 qt.) saucepan. Reduce to a simmer and cook, stirring occasionally, until the quinoa is tender, about 15 minutes. Meanwhile place the almonds in a small skillet and cook over medium heat until starting to turn golden. Keep an eye on them! Set almonds aside.

In a medium bowl, whisk 1 ½ cups milk, eggs, raisins, brown sugar, cinnamon, nutmeg, and salt together until well mixed. Slowly pour into the quinoa mixture while whisking to combine. Bring to a simmer and cook for 5 minutes, stirring frequently. Pour the pudding into a large bowl and cool slightly. Place plastic wrap so that it touches the surface of the pudding and refrigerate to chill*. Spoon into individual serving bowls, sprinkle with almonds and enjoy.

*Note: If you would like, you can eat some while warm - it will just be more like cereal and milk. The cooled dish is more like a porridge.

Muffin-Shaped Eggs and (Homemade) Turkey Sausage

....

Makes 10 "muffins".

These look just like muffins, but they're actually a fun and delicious egg and sausage creation! For the milk in the recipe, 1% or 2% is probably ideal, but skim is fine.

For the sausage:

1/2 lb. ground turkey, half dark meat (thighs) and half breast, if possible

1 1/2 Tbsp. fresh sage, chopped

1 Tbsp. parsley, chopped

1 garlic clove, minced

1/8 tsp. dried red pepper flakes, optional

1/8 tsp. Kosher salt

1/8 tsp. pepper

1 tsp. olive oil

Egg mixture:

8 eggs, minus 2 yolks (can see HELPING HAND for how to separate eggs)

2 Tbsp. milk

1/4 tsp. salt

1/2 cup shredded cheddar cheese (the lower fat variety actually tastes pretty good), packed down

Preheat the oven to 350 degrees.

Spray a muffin tin with Pam.

In a medium skillet over medium heat, begin to brown the turkey, and cook for about 5 minutes. Stir occasionally with a wooden spoon. Drain any fat by pouring the meat into a colander over the sink. Return the meat to the skillet. While the heat is on medium, add the sage, parsley, garlic, red pepper flakes, if using, salt, pepper, and 1 tsp. olive oil. Cook for 2 minutes more while stirring. Set aside.

In a medium bowl, whisk the eggs and milk until well mixed. Stir in the salt. Stir in the sausage and cheese.

Spoon into your prepared muffin tin (I use a soup ladle), filling them about ¾ full. Bake for 18-20 minutes, or until a knife inserted near the center comes out clean.

Addictive Homemade Granola

....

Serves 8.

Your friends are going to ask for the recipe, or beg you to make more! If you want to add seeds such as sesame (toasted or not) or flax, add those when you add the dried fruit so the seeds don't burn. By the way, for my Jewish friends, this makes a totally delicious granola for Passover- just substitute whole grain farfel for the oats in the recipe.

½ cup light or dark brown sugar, packed

½ cup water

¼ cup canola oil

3 Tbsp. butter

½ cup sliced almonds

½ cup sweetened shredded coconut

1 tsp. cinnamon

12 oz. oats (not the quick cooking kind), about 4 cups

1/3 to ½ cup diced dried apricots, or dried fruit of your choice

Preheat the oven to 350 degrees.

Cover a rimmed baking sheet with aluminum foil.
Spray the foil with Pam.

Put the sugar, water, oil and butter in a large saucepan over medium heat. Stir until the butter melts. Stir in the almonds, coconut, and cinnamon. Add the oats and stir until well combined. Spread the granola on the prepared pan. Bake 15 minutes. Stir: I take a regular soup spoon and gently move the granola on the outer edges, which brown first, in toward the middle. Then I spread it out again. Cook about 10 minutes more, or until it is as golden as you like it (I like it pretty golden - gives it a great crunch!) Remove from the oven and sprinkle the apricots over the top. Cool. Mix together with your fingers.

Cool completely and store any leftovers in an airtight container. This granola freezes very well.

High Protein Chocolate Smoothie

....

Serves 1.

This is my go-to protein smoothie. So healthy, yet so delicious!

A few thoughts on smoothies: It's great if you get in the habit of keeping some frozen bananas around- they are tasty, and throwing one into your smoothie will give it some extra thickness and chill. Also, liquid goes in the blender first. Totally use your imagination with smoothie ingredient possibilities like fruit, juices, yogurt, wheat germ, flax seeds, almonds, bee pollen, oat bran, and leafy greens like kale, collard greens, and spinach.

½ cup milk (I use 1%)

1 scoop good quality vanilla flavor whey protein powder

12 almonds (unsalted), preferably raw

½ medium banana (frozen if you have one handy), broken in half

4 ice cubes

1 tsp. turbinado ("in the raw") sugar

1 tsp. unsweetened cocoa powder

Blend and enjoy!

All happiness depends on a leisurely breakfast.

– John Gunther

Tis an ill cook that cannot lick his own fingers.

- Shakespeare, Romeo and Juliet

BEFORE YOU DIG IN

whet your appetite

Tomatoes with Bleu Cheese, Pine Nuts, and Basil

....

Serves 4.

It sounds fancy, but the prep isn't. I love a fresh, ripe tomato and this appetizer would certainly be a star in the summertime when tomatoes are at their best. Not only do the flavors marry well; this dish gets a high rating for presentation!

4 medium tomatoes (on the ripe side)

3 Tbsp. crumbled bleu cheese

2 Tbsp. pine nuts, toasted

4 large basil leaves, sliced chiffonade style (see HELPING HAND)

1 ½ tsp. good balsamic vinegar

1 ½ tsp. olive oil

Pinch Kosher salt

Sprinkle of pepper

Slice the tomatoes and arrange the slices on a serving plate. To toast the pine nuts, just put them in a small pan and cook over medium heat until fragrant. Stir every once in a while so not just one side turns golden. Resist the temptation to walk away and do something else—they'll surprise you very quickly and burn!

Top the tomatoes with a fairly even sprinkling of the bleu cheese, pine nuts and basil. Finish with a drizzle of olive oil and balsamic vinegar, and a sprinkle of salt and pepper.

Beauty.

Toasted Parmesan Eggplant "Chips"

Serves 4.

One day, I had extra baked eggplant slices when making eggplant parmesan. I asked my son if he wanted some, and he asked if we had any marinara sauce (which we happened to have). The idea of including this recipe as an appetizer was born. Since they are made in the oven and eggplant is a veritable oil sponge when fried in a pan, these are a healthy pleasure.

1 medium eggplant

3 Tbsp. olive oil for brushing

1/3 cup grated parmesan cheese

Set the oven to broil and place the oven rack under the broiler.

Spray a cookie sheet with Pam. Have a pastry brush ready to use.

Optional: Marinara sauce for dipping (store bought variety with few ingredients starting with tomatoes, no corn syrup, and little, if any, sugar)

Peel the eggplant (can see HELPING HAND) and slice crosswise into about ½ inch circles. You want them not too thin - or they might get too crispy and not lift easily off of the pan - but not too thick, so they remain a delicate bite.

Place the slices on the cookie sheet, pour the olive oil into a small container and brush both sides of each slice lightly with olive oil. Cook under the broiler in the oven until golden on top. It doesn't take long-maybe 4-6 minutes or so, depending on your oven. Take the cookie sheet out and flip the eggplant slices. Top each slice with a sprinkling of parmesan cheese. Place in the oven and cook until golden, about 4 minutes.

Meanwhile warm the marinara, if using (either in the microwave or on the stove). Dip and enjoy!

Cannellini Bean Dip with Green Chiles and Figs

Serves 6.

Cannellini Beans are very popular in Central and Southern Italy, particularly in Tuscany. They have a buttery texture and nutty flavor- perfect for a healthy dip to start your meal. I love how their flavor takes on the green chiles and the dried figs. The leftover chiles would be great in scrambled eggs! Also, you can freeze the whole rosemary sprigs and save for a later use.

1 14 oz. can Cannellini beans, rinsed and drained

1 Tbsp. chopped red onion

1 ½ tsp. minced fresh rosemary (the leaves come off easily if you hold a sprig at the top with one hand and zip your other hand down the sprig)

1 Tbsp. fresh lemon juice

1/8 cup water

½ tsp. fresh lemon zest (only the yellow part of the skin), minced

1 ½ tsp. olive oil

¼ tsp. Kosher salt

¼ tsp. pepper

2 Tbsp. chopped green chiles

4 dried Mission figs, chopped (cut into quarters, lengthwise, and chop into small pieces)

Serve with: Whole grain pita triangles or Ciabatta bread

If you have a food processor, add all of the ingredients, except the figs, to the bowl and process until smooth. Transfer to a serving bowl, add the figs, and stir.

If you don't have a food processor, mash the beans with a fork on your cutting board or sheet. Transfer to a mixing bowl. Add the remaining ingredients and stir until well combined.

Spiced Falafel Spread and Homemade Tzatziki Sauce

Serves 6.

Falafel is an iconic part of Israeli cuisine and is a very popular fast food in the Middle East. It's main ingredient is ground chickpeas, which have a great nutritional profile. The falafel is traditionally deep fried and served in pita bread with salads and tahini (sesame paste) based sauces. My inspiration for this dish is that I love great falafel. That, and the fact that I wanted to make it delicious, but not fried. A homemade tzatziki sauce adds the perfect finishing touch, both for flavor and presentation!

You'll need a food processor for this dish.

For the spread:

14 oz. can chickpeas, rinsed and drained

2 small scallions, chopped (white and green parts)

2 cloves garlic, minced

1 ½ tsp. cumin

2 tsp. coriander

¼ tsp. Kosher salt

¼ tsp. cayenne pepper

Juice of ½ medium lemon

4 Tbsp. minced parsley

¼ cup water

2 Tbsp. olive oil

For the Tzatziki sauce:

1 cup fat free plain Greek yogurt

¼ cup English cucumber, diced small*

1 ½ tsp. white vinegar

1 tsp. fresh lemon juice

½ tsp. finely minced garlic

1 ½ tsp. olive oil

¼ tsp. Kosher salt

Pinch pepper

Serve with: Pita bread and cucumber slices
Garnish: sprinkling of paprika

For the falafel spread, place the chickpeas and remaining ingredients in your food processor and process until smooth.

Transfer to a bowl.

For the sauce, combine all the ingredients in a medium bowl and stir to combine.

Cut the pita bread into triangles and spread with falafel. Top with a thin slice of cucumber and a dollop of tzatziki. Sprinkle with paprika. Beauty!

Note: While English cucumbers don't tend to have many seeds, for this recipe it's best to cut most them out and discard.

Warm Spinach Artichoke Dip

....

Serves 4-6.

There are so many versions of Spinach Artichoke Dip out there, and I think too many of them are lacking in texture, boldness of flavor, and rely on extra mayonnaise to carry them. Since this dish is one of my family's favorites, we have lots of sampling history! This healthier-than-most recipe has come out on top for us and our friends!

1 10 oz. box of frozen chopped spinach, thawed and squeezed dry

1 (14 oz.) can artichoke hearts (not the marinated kind), drained and chopped

4 oz. shredded mozzarella cheese

1/2 cup mayonnaise (I prefer Hellman's)

1 cup grated parmesan cheese

¼ tsp. garlic salt

¼ tsp. pepper

Preheat the oven to 350 degrees.

Spray an 8x8 baking dish with Pam.

Put the spinach in a glass microwave safe container (I use the 8x8 glass dish I'm going to bake in). Add ¼ cup water and cook for 5 minutes. Let the spinach cool somewhat —it helps to spread it out with a fork- or put it in the fridge for a few minutes. When it is cool enough to handle, take some spinach in your hands and, over the sink, squeeze out as much water as you can. Break up the "ball" of spinach as you put it in a medium bowl (this just makes it easier to stir the rest of the ingredients in later). Continue until all the spinach has been squeezed and put in the bowl.

Add the remaining ingredients and stir to mix well. Put the mixture in the baking dish. Bake 25 minutes or until it is bubbling around the edges.

Serve with:

Tortilla chips (there are some whole grain/lower fat ones out there that are truly tasty)- maybe ones with a hint of lime.

A salsa of your choice

Note: If you want a healthy and crunchy alternative to chips, try veggie dippers like celery, carrots, red peppers, or jicama (can see HELPING HAND re: jicama).

Homemade Fresh Tomato Salsa

Serves 4-6.

You'll impress people with this. And, you'll enjoy the extra fresh taste of salsa that's not from a grocery store shelf! It takes a bit of time to dice the tomatoes, but it's worth it. If you can make the salsa a bit ahead of time, the flavors will have a nice chance to blend together.

4 medium tomatoes (fairly ripe), seeded (can see HELPING HAND) and diced small

3 Tbsp. minced onion

¼ cup parsley, minced

Juice of one small lime

1 small fresh jalapeno, seeded and minced (more- or less-depending on how much heat you like)

2 garlic cloves, minced

¼ tsp. salt

½ tsp. pepper

To seed the jalapeno, cut the pepper lengthwise, and with the end of a knife, scrape the seeds out.

Gently combine all the ingredients together in a serving bowl.

Serve with:

Tortilla chips (there are some baked and whole grain varieties that are actually good!). Also, the salsa goes really well with Warm Spinach Artichoke Dip.

Parmesan Stuffed Mushrooms

....

Serves 4.

Our friends and family love these mushrooms and they are one of our son Benjy's favorites. While stuffed mushrooms are popular restaurant fare, I often find that the star ingredient is soggy breadcrumbs! This recipe includes the delicious flavors of garlic, butter, and parmesan cheese, yet manages to stay in the healthy category. Honestly, whenever I serve them, they never last long!

Have a baking dish large enough for the mushrooms ready to use.

12 medium mushrooms (the regular white variety)

2 Tbsp. olive oil, divided

½ small onion, minced

2 garlic cloves, minced

1/3 cup grated Parmesan cheese

2 Tbsp. parsley, minced

1 Tbsp. butter, melted

Wipe the mushrooms with a damp towel. Slice the very end off of the mushroom stems and discard. Take the stems out (twist slightly and apply a little pressure at the base and they should pop out pretty easily). Finely chop the stems and set aside. Prepare the onion, garlic, and parsley and set aside.

Heat 1 Tbsp. olive oil in a medium skillet on medium heat. Swirl to coat the bottom of the skillet and add the whole mushrooms, stem side up. Cook until slightly golden, about 4-5 minutes. Then, flip and cook on medium-high heat for 1-2 minutes, until softened. Remove from the skillet and place in a baking dish, with the stem sides up (ready to be stuffed).

For the stuffing:

Wipe the skillet with a damp paper towel. Heat 1 Tbsp. olive oil over medium heat. Add the onions and cook for about 1-2 minutes (until translucent). Add the garlic and mushroom stem pieces. Cook until onions are just slightly golden, stirring occasionally. Transfer to a small bowl and add the cheese, parsley and butter. Stir well to moisten.

Stuff the mushroom caps (I use my fingers; you can use a small spoon if you wish). Put the mushrooms in the oven set to broil just before you want to serve. They are ready when the top is sizzling a bit. It won't take long, so keep an eye on them! You just want them nice and hot.

Classic Hummus

....

Serves 6.

Hummus is a Middle Eastern dip made from chickpeas and tahini (paste made from sesame seeds similar in texture to peanut butter) dating back to ancient Egypt. It's truly delicious and a great source of fiber, protein, and other beneficial vitamins and minerals.

Hummus is definitely a dish that lends itself to creativity. Over the years, I have enjoyed garlic, sundried tomato, roasted red pepper, lemon thyme, kalamata olive, and even edamame hummus. However, my favorite is still the classic version. Once you make this, you may never want store-bought hummus again! Refrigerate any leftovers.

You'll need a food processor for this recipe.

4 garlic cloves

14 oz. can chickpeas (garbanzo beans) with few added ingredients, rinsed and drained- about 2 cups

½ tsp. Kosher salt

1/3 cup tahini (sesame paste)

3 Tbsp. fresh lemon juice

2 tbsp. water

2 Tbsp. olive oil

¼ tsp. cumin

Optional Garnishes: paprika, chopped parsley, chopped tomato, a few whole chickpeas, and/or a drizzle of olive oil

Put the garlic in your food processor fitted with a steel blade. Process until it is minced. Add the remaining ingredients and process until smooth. Transfer to your serving bowl.

Serve with: fresh veggie (e.g. carrots, celery, jicama, red or yellow peppers, cucumbers) spears, whole wheat pita wedges and/or some olives on the side.

Go-To Guacamole

....

Serves 4.

My family sure appreciates the avocado! And we love our "guac." There's usually a great excuse to make guacamole: have it with Good Ole Chili, with No Tortilla Chicken Enchiladas, with Tommy's Tacos, or just with good quality corn chips.

2 large ripe avocados, mashed (can see HELPING HAND for Selecting and Preparing)

1 ½ Tbsp. fresh lemon juice

1/4 tsp. garlic powder

1/4 tsp. onion powder

1/4 tsp. chili powder

1/4 tsp. salt

1/4 tsp. pepper

Optional: 1 medium tomato, diced

Slice the avocados, lengthwise, all the way around. Separate the halves. Remove the pit, and scoop out the meat of the fruit. Mash the avocados (smushing them with a whisk works well!) in a medium size bowl. Add the rest of the ingredients and mix well. Taste and adjust lemon juice and/or salt to your liking if necessary. Add the tomatoes, if using, and mix gently to combine.

If you are not going to eat right away, keep the avocado pit, place it inside your mixed guacamole, and cover with plastic wrap. That will reduce browning while the guac waits to be consumed!

Crunchy Spiced Kale Chips

....

Serves 4.

Kale is a super food full of powerful antioxidants, and a great source of Vitamins A and C. The kale chips in a plastic bag that I saw at the store just didn't seem appealing to me. So, I decided to see how fresh kale would translate to chips in my own kitchen. They were impossibly light, super crunchy, and had a really nice depth of flavor. Our dinner guests parked near the bowl and ate 'til the chips were gone. Since the experiment worked, I knew I must remember to make more next time! This recipe is super easy and the answer for pre-meal snacking!

1 large bunch of kale (can see HELPING HAND for How to Select)

1 1/2 Tbsp. olive oil

¼ tsp. garlic powder

¼ tsp. chili powder

1/8 tsp. pepper

Scant 1/4 tsp. Kosher salt (or to taste)

Preheat the oven to 350 degrees.

Spray a rimmed baking sheet with Pam.

Wash the kale. Remove the leaves from the tough stems by folding the leaves in half lengthwise and cutting the stems off. Discard the stems.

Cut or tear the leaves into "chip" size pieces. Dry the kale well in your salad spinner and transfer to a large bowl. Drizzle the olive oil over the kale and add the spices. "Massage" the leaves with your fingers until they are lightly coated with oil and the spices are distributed. Place in one layer (try not to overlap) on your baking sheet. Cook for 11-13 minutes, gently tossing once during cooking, until crunchy (the edges are brown but are not burnt). Gently gather the kale and transfer to a serving plate. Enjoy!

Ultimate Deviled Eggs

....

Makes 12.

If you're a deviled eggs fan, you'll appreciate how easy these are to make. This is the classic at its best, but there are so many ways you can tweak deviled eggs. Just a few possible additions are chopped green olives, prepared horseradish, fresh dill, or sun dried tomatoes. Of course, you're not limited to a single added ingredient!

6 eggs

4 Tbsp. mayonnaise (I prefer Hellman's)

2 Tbsp. dill pickles, minced

1 1/4 tsp. white vinegar

1/8 tsp. salt

1/8 tsp. pepper

Pinch of cayenne pepper if you like a little kick

Garnish: Sprinkle of paprika

Hard boil the eggs (can see HELPING HAND). Peel and slice the eggs lengthwise. Gently remove the yolks and place in a bowl. Place the whites on your serving plate. Mash the yolks with a fork or a whisk. Add the remaining ingredients and mix well with a spoon (until creamy). Use a small spoon to fill the whites with the yolk mixture. Sprinkle with paprika, if using.

Baked Tofu Squares

....

Serves 6.

For tofu lovers and those who think they hate tofu (!), this recipe is worth a try. Effort on your part is very minimal, but plan ahead a bit since it takes about an hour to an hour and a half for the tofu to drain, marinate and bake. The tofu squares are tasty on their own, and would be great in a salad (try spinach, red onion, egg, toasted almonds, and the tofu squares- with a citrus vinaigrette), a stir fry, or a whole wheat pasta and veggie dish.

16 oz. container extra firm tofu, cut into 1 inch squares

For the marinade:

3 Tbsp. reduced sodium soy sauce

2 Tbsp. pure maple syrup

1 tsp. sesame oil

1 Tbsp. lemon juice

2 tsp. rice vinegar or apple cider vinegar

Pinch ground ginger

1 tsp. hot sauce (I used 1 tsp. of Sriracha Chili Sauce, and they come out with a hint of spice)

Drain and quickly rinse the block of tofu. In order to remove much of the moisture (so it can better absorb the marinade), put the tofu on a rimmed dinner plate, with some paper towels underneath it. Cover with more towels. Carefully place a plate or other weight on top of the towels to press down on the tofu. Let it sit at least 15 minutes. To remove even more moisture, change the towels and let it sit another 15 minutes.

Whisk the marinade ingredients together in a small bowl. Set aside.

Cut the tofu into 1 inch squares. I cut the block in half, make a few horizontal slices, and then cube. Put the tofu in a shallow container, cover with marinade, and let sit for between 15 minutes and 30 minutes (the longer it sits, the more intense the flavor will be). Flip the tofu a few times so the marinade is absorbed evenly.

Preheat the oven to 350 degrees. Line a baking sheet with foil and spray with Pam.

Transfer the tofu to your baking sheet and cook, turning once, for about 30 minutes, 'til they have firmed up and are golden.

Worries go down better with soup.

- A Jewish Proverb

cozy SOUPS

Butternut Squash Soup with Sage and Cranberries

....

Serves 4.

Butternut squash conjures up my favorite time of the year. It's the time for acorns and pumpkins, deep green leaves back-lit by patches of chartreuse, orange, and red, and crunchy walking through leaves yet to be raked.

Lots of people must share my enthusiasm about butternut squash soup since so many restaurant menus feature it. But it's so nice to be able to make this treat at home where you control the ingredients. There's no need for a food proces-sor, and no pureeing of hot messy liquid in this recipe! Ever so slightly sweet, and supremely satisfying…

As for the butternut squash, it can be really tough to cut through unless your knives are good. Even then, it requires great care. I don't mean to scare you, just to remind you to be careful. The most important thing to consider is to keep whatever pieces you are working with as stable as possible.

Plan ahead since the butternut squash roasts for about 40 minutes. And, for a vegetarian soup, use vegetable broth instead of chicken.

1 large head garlic (not "elephant" garlic)

1 butternut squash (about 2 ½ lbs.), halved lengthwise

1 Tbsp. butter

1 Tbsp. olive oil, plus 1 1/2 tsp. for drizzling over garlic and squash

1 small onion, diced

2 carrots, peeled and diced small

3 cups chicken stock (mostly fat free is pretty easy to find – or vegetable stock to make the soup vegetarian)

3/4 tsp. Kosher salt

¼ tsp. pepper

1 1/2 Tbsp. fresh sage, chopped

¼ tsp. red chili flakes, optional

½ cup plain fat free Greek yogurt

Garnish: Top each bowl of soup with a sprinkling of dried cranberries.*

Preheat the oven to 400 degrees.

Spray a rimmed baking sheet with Pam.

Prepare your garlic: leave the paper-y skin on and cut off about ½ inch of the pointed top of the head, so that most of the cloves are exposed. Place the garlic in some foil, drizzle with ½ tsp. olive oil, seal the foil like a pouch, and it's ready for the oven. Set aside.

Slice the stem off of the top of the squash and slice off the bottom. Stand the squash upright on a cutting board. It shouldn't wobble; you want the squash to be stable (if it is wobbly, make another cut at the bottom to even it out). Make one long cut, down the middle from the top to bottom, with a heavy chef's knife. To help with the cutting you can use a rubber mallet to gently tap on the ends of the knife to help push the knife down through the squash.

Also, if the neck is too crooked to make one cut, slice off at the crook, and halve that part separately.

Using a spoon, scoop out and discard the seeds and fi-brous strings. Place on your prepared baking sheet, cut side up. Use 1 tsp. of olive oil and drizzle over the squash. Rub around with your fingers. Place the garlic foil pouch on the baking sheet as well.

Cook the squash and garlic for 40-45 minutes, until quite tender (for the squash, soft, like a baked potato would feel when ready. To check, I use a kitchen towel to protect my hands, and give it a little squeeze).

While the squash and garlic are cooling, melt the butter and olive oil in a large saucepan over medium heat. Add the on-ion and carrots and cook for 6-8 minutes, stirring occasion-ally, until the veggies are softened. Add the stock, salt, pep-per, sage, and red chili flakes, if using.

When the garlic and squash are cool enough to handle, un-wrap the garlic and squeeze the cloves into a large bowl. Mash them with a fork.

Scoop the squash pulp out with a spoon. Note that if you turn the squash upside down, the skin will peel off pretty easily. Add the squash to the garlic, and mash (with a potato masher, whisk, or fork).

Add the mashed squash and the garlic to the soup mixture and whisk to combine well. Whisk the Greek yogurt into the soup until well combined. Warm thoroughly (don't let it boil), and serve with a sprinkle of dried cranberries. For looks, you can float a whole sage leaf on top of each serving. Enjoy.

* Note: One of my recipe testers topped the soup with some shaved parmesan cheese too and loved the nutty, salty finish.

Grandma's Chicken Soup

....

Serves 6.

Restaurant and store bought chicken soup doesn't always live up to its reputation as a comfort food extraordinaire. But my husband's grandmother's recipe does! It's hard to go wrong with her wholesome, homemade version. While it's actually very easy to make, it takes a while to develop the delicious flavor so plan ahead.

1 whole chicken (organic if you can)

4 celery stalks, chopped

3 medium carrots, chopped

1 medium-large onion, chopped

4 Tbsp. parsley, minced

14 oz. can chicken broth (mostly fat free is pretty easy to find)

½ tsp. Kosher salt

½ tsp. pepper

2/3 of a 16 oz. bag of thin egg noodles, optional

Take any extra fat off the chicken (look near the front of the cavity and at the back end of the chicken). Rinse the chicken, inside and out. Put in a large soup pot and cover with water. Add the vegetables and parsley, and bring to a boil. Turn the heat to a simmer and cook for about 1 ½ hours. Every once in a while skim the "scum" off the top with a large spoon, and discard. I have found that when I use an organic chicken, much less stuff rises to the top.

Take the chicken out of the pot (you can use a fork and a big spoon to lift- the spoon inside the cavity and the fork at the rear), tilting it downward a little so the liquid flows into the pot, and place in a large bowl. Let the chicken cool until you can handle it.

Begin to season up the soup: add the broth and the salt and pepper. Stir and taste the soup. It may need some more salt/ pepper. Remove the chicken meat from the bones, chop as necessary so that they are bite size, and add to the pot.

Bring the soup to a simmer, add the noodles, if using, and cook for about 10 minutes, until the noodles are done. You want them to be tender, but still have a little a "bite" (al dente!).

Enjoy!

Tortilla Soup Especiale

....

Serves 4-6.

This is a great soup in cold weather and the flavors of the broth, corn, onions, garlic, tomatoes, and spices just seem meant for each other! There are hundreds of ways to adapt this recipe based on your personal preferences. If you want it vegetarian and are after a one dish meal, use only vegetable broth and consider adding a fried egg. If you want some greens, you can add some shredded spinach or Swiss chard. Just a couple of possibilities!

For the tortilla matchsticks:

Three 6-inch corn tortillas (with few ingredients)

Pam to spray the sticks

Sprinkle of paprika

For the soup:

1 Tbsp. Canola oil

Four 6-inch corn tortillas (with few ingredients), cut into small (about 1") squares

1 small onion, diced

1 medium to large Poblano pepper, seeded (can see HELP-ING HAND) and diced

3 good sized cloves garlic, minced

14 ½ oz. can diced tomatoes with mild chilies

2 (14 ½ oz.) cans vegetable broth

14 ½ oz. can chicken broth (mostly fat free is pretty easy to find, or use vegetable broth to make the soup vegetarian)

¾ tsp. chili powder

¾ tsp. ground cumin

¼ tsp. pepper

1 cup frozen corn, mostly thawed

1 ½-2 Tbsp. fresh lime juice (to taste)

1 large ripe avocado, peeled and diced

Optional: 3 skinless, boneless chicken breasts OR about 3 cups of cooked chicken breast from a store bought rotisserie chicken, chopped

Preheat the oven to 350. Cut 3 tortillas in half and then into matchstick-thin strips. Spread out on a baking sheet and spray with Pam. Sprinkle with a bit of paprika, give them a toss, and spread out again. Bake for about 10 minutes or until golden and crispy. Set aside.

Heat the oil over medium heat in a large saucepan. Add the tortilla pieces and cook, stirring occasionally, for about 10 minutes, or until they start to turn golden. Add the onion and Poblano pepper. Cook for 5 minutes, stirring occasionally. Add garlic and cook for another minute while stirring. Add the tomatoes, vegetable and chicken broths, chili powder, cumin and pepper. Bring to a boil, then lower the heat to a simmer and cook for 15 minutes (see below if you are going to add chicken). Add the corn. Bring to a simmer and cook for 5 minutes. Remove the pot from the heat, add the lime juice, and stir. Place in serving bowls, top each with diced avocado and tortilla matchsticks, and enjoy!

If you are adding chicken, before you add the corn:

For uncooked chicken: Prep the chicken (see HELPING HAND) and chop into roughly bite size chunks. Add to the soup. Stir, bring to a boil, and lower the heat to a simmer. Cook for about 15 minutes. Check the chicken for doneness by cutting through one of the thickest pieces and making sure it is not pink inside. Add the corn. Bring to a simmer and cook for 5 minutes. Remove the pot from the heat, add the lime juice, and stir. Place in serving bowls, and top each with diced avocado and tortilla matchsticks.

For cooked chicken: Add the chicken to the soup, stir and simmer for about 5-6 minutes or until the chicken is heated through. Add the corn. Bring to a simmer and cook for 5 minutes. Remove the pot from the heat, add the lime juice, and stir. Place in serving bowls, and top each with diced avocado and tortilla matchsticks.

Little Italy Tomato Soup

....

Serves 6.

As the weather cools and warm foods beckon, there's nothing like a bowl of hot soup to help you shake off the worries of the day. My tomato soup has great flavor and texture going on, as well as a protein boost from the butter-y white beans. So, have some friends over and enjoy this with a simple green salad and a hunk of crusty whole grain bread topped with melted cheese.

1 Tbsp. Olive oil

1 large onion, diced

2 carrots, diced small

4 cloves garlic, minced

1 28 oz. can crushed tomatoes (I like San Marzano or Cento brand)

1 28 oz. can Italian plum tomatoes, without the juice (give the tomatoes a gentle-to avoid splashing- crush with your hand as you put them in the pot)

1 cup chicken or vegetable broth (mostly fat free is pretty easy to find)

1/2 tsp. sugar

1 1/2 tsp. Kosher salt

¼ tsp. pepper

½ tsp. red pepper flakes (less if you prefer)

1 ½ tsp. balsamic vinegar (preferably a good one)

15 oz. can white beans (such as Canellini or Great Northern), rinsed and drained

½ cup grated parmesan cheese

Optional garnish: top each bowl with a little shaved or grated parmesan cheese and a fresh basil leaf.

Heat the oil in a large saucepan over medium heat. Add the onions and carrots and stir. Cook on medium heat until the veggies start to soften, about 7-8 minutes. Stir occasionally. Add the garlic and cook for another minute, while stirring. Add the tomatoes, chicken or vegetable broth, sugar, salt, pepper, crushed red pepper flakes, and balsamic vinegar. Stir and bring to a boil. Add the beans, stir, and bring to a boil again. Reduce the heat to a simmer, cover the pot partway (to avoid splattering) and cook for 20 minutes. Stir the ½ cup of parmesan cheese into the soup until incorporated.

Delish!

Kale and Kidney Bean Soup

....

Serves 6.

This soup is beautiful and delicious! Kale is one of the healthiest vegetables around. With an earthy flavor, it is particularly awesome in soups, or wilted on the stove with some garlic, and finished with a little balsamic vinegar. I particularly love the addition of some golden raisins to this soup for a little sweet surprise. Pair this soup with a warm, whole grain, crusty bread for a great lunch or dinner.

4 cups kale (packed down), rinsed and chopped (can see HELPING HAND for Selecting) - 1 bunch should do it

1 1/2 Tbsp. olive oil

1 small onion, diced

4 cloves garlic, minced

4 cups vegetable or chicken stock (mostly fat free is pretty easy to find)

15 oz. can diced tomatoes (with few added ingredients)

15 oz. can kidney beans, rinsed and drained

1 cup frozen sweet corn, mostly thawed (can use the microwave)

½ tsp. turmeric

1 tsp. Kosher salt

¼ tsp. pepper

2 Tbsp. fresh lemon juice

Optional: 3 Tbsp. golden raisins

Take your corn out and set aside.

Wash the kale. Remove the leaves from the tough stems by folding the leaves in half lengthwise and cutting the stems off with a knife (or use kitchen shears). Discard the stems. To chop, stack the leaves, cut into thin ribbons, and then cut cross wise (into bite size pieces).

Prep your onion and garlic, and rinse and drain the beans.

Heat a large saucepan over medium heat. Add the olive oil and onion. Cook for about 4 minutes, stirring occasionally, until soft (don't let it brown). Add the garlic and cook about 1 minute, while stirring. Add the stock, tomatoes, beans, corn, kale, turmeric, salt and pepper. Stir and raise heat to med-high to bring to a boil. Lower the heat to a simmer. Cover the pot, and then just slide the top off a bit, leaving some room for steam to escape. Simmer for 25 minutes. Remove the pot from the heat, add the lemon juice and raisins, if using. Stir, cover the pot and let sit for 5 minutes.

Enjoy!

Cioppino (Fish Stew)

....

Serves 4-6.

Cioppino is an Italian fish stew that originated in San Francisco. While classically it is made with a combination of shrimp, fish and shellfish, there are many ways to go with this recipe. I have chosen to use different types of fish. It's delicious, filling, and warming. How can you go wrong? A warm loaf of sourdough bread would be awesome with this...

1 Tbsp. olive oil

1 large sweet onion, diced

1 medium carrot, diced small

4 large garlic cloves, minced

28 oz. can diced tomatoes (with few added ingredients), with juice

1/2 tsp. salt

1/4 tsp. oregano

1/4 tsp. turmeric

1/4 tsp. crushed red pepper flakes (less if you like less heat)

2 heaping Tbsp. tomato paste

1 Tbsp. balsamic vinegar (preferably a good one)

4 cups fish or vegetable stock (preferably fish)

1 ¾ -2 lbs. fish- any combination of salmon, mahi mahi, cod, halibut, red snapper, cut into more or less bite size pieces

Heat a large saucepan/soup pot over medium heat. Add the olive oil, onions, and carrots. Cook until the onions are translucent, about 5-6 minutes. Stir occasionally. Add the garlic, and cook, stirring, about 2 minutes more. Add the tomatoes and the remaining ingredients, except for the fish. Stir to combine and bring to a boil. Add the fish, and cook at a simmer (low boil) for 30 minutes.

Enjoy!

Green Chile Soup with Chicken

....

Serves 4.

My husband and I had lunch one afternoon at one of our favorite restaurants in Hood River, Oregon, and I decided to come up with my own version of their "soup of the day" that combined chicken and green chiles. This soup is especially great on an afternoon when you're just feeling like warming up from the inside! It's wholesome and light, but very satisfying.

1 Tbsp. olive oil

¾ cup chopped onion

2 stalks celery, chopped (about ¼ inch slices)

4 garlic cloves, minced

6 cups chicken broth (mostly fat free is pretty easy to find)

2 (4 oz.) cans diced green chiles

1/8 tsp. crushed red pepper flakes

1/2 tsp. Kosher salt

1 ½ lb. chicken breast tenders, chopped into bite size pieces

Juice of ½ small lime (about 1 Tbsp.)

3 Tbsp. cilantro, chopped

Prep your onion, celery, and garlic. Heat the olive oil in a large saucepan, over medium heat. Add the onion and celery, stir, and cook until softened, about 7-8 minutes. Stir occasionally. Add the garlic, and cook for another minute, while stirring. Add the chicken broth, chiles, red pepper flakes, and salt. Stir and bring to a boil. Add the chicken pieces, stir, and bring to a simmer (slow boil). Cook until the chicken is cooked through (no longer pink inside), about 12 minutes. Remove the pot from the heat, stir in the lime juice and the cilantro, and serve.

Silky Corn Chowder

....

Serves 4.

This chowder served with a fresh green salad makes a perfect light meal. It tastes like you worked hard, but it's actually kind of fun to make!

Since my husband and son love corn chowder, I try to make the most of sweet, fresh summer corn. But, if corn isn't in season, you can make this with frozen corn and still enjoy a taste of summer.

3 ears of corn, kernels removed (about 1 ½ to 2 cups)- see below for technique

2 medium potatoes, diced small (1/2" cubes)—I like Yukon Gold

1 Tbsp. olive oil

½ medium onion, diced

2 cloves garlic, minced

3 cups low fat (1%) milk

½ tsp. Kosher salt

¼ tsp. pepper

¼ tsp. paprika

½ tsp. curry powder

½ small jalapeno, seeded (can see HELPING HAND) and diced, optional

Peel the outer leaves off of the corn. Stand each ear on its wide end on a cutting board or your plastic cutting sheet. While holding the top, use a serrated knife to carefully cut the kernels off the cob with a downward motion. Keep going all the way around each ear of corn. Set the kernels aside.

Place the potatoes (no need to peel) in a large soup pot, with water to cover. Bring to a boil. Lower the heat to a simmer and cook until the potatoes are fork tender, about 12 minutes.

Prep your onions and garlic, and set aside. Heat a small saucepan over medium heat. Add the olive oil and the onions. Cook until the onions are translucent, about 4-6 minutes, stirring occasionally. Add the garlic , stir, and cook until fragrant, about 1 minute.

Add the onion mixture, corn, milk, salt, pepper, paprika, curry powder, and jalapeno, if using, to the potatoes. Stir and cook at a low boil for 10 minutes.

Split Pea Soup with Sausage and Sweet Potatoes

....

Serves 6.

If you like pea soup, I think you'll love the earthy flavors and the addition of sausage and sweet potatoes in this recipe. If you don't like pea soup, this soup might just turn you into a fan! It's tasty, healthy, and hearty. That has to count for something! Plan ahead a bit since the soup takes about an hour to cook.

2 cups dry green split peas*, sorted through to make sure there are no pebbles, rinsed, and drained (use a small colander)

12 oz. to 1 lb. "fully cooked" turkey sausage (with simple, pronounce-able ingredients) , sliced in half length-wise

1 medium sweet potato, peeled and cut into small (roughly 1") cubes

1 Tbsp. olive oil

1 medium onion, chopped

2 carrots, diced

2 stalks celery, diced

3/4 tsp. Kosher salt

¼ tsp. pepper

¼ tsp. cumin

4 cups chicken broth (mostly fat free is pretty easy to find)

3 cups water

Juice of 1/2 lemon

* Note: Try to buy bright green peas. Lighter colored ones will have less flavor.

Prepare the peas. In a medium skillet, over medium heat, cook the sausage until golden on both sides. Set aside. Prep your sweet potatoes so they are ready to go.

Heat a large stock/soup pot over medium heat. Add the olive oil, onions, carrots, celery, salt, pepper, and cumin. Give it a stir. Cook until the veggies start to soften, 6- 8 minutes. Stir occasionally. Cut the sausage into bite size pieces.

Add the peas, sausage, sweet potatoes, broth, and water to the soup pot. Bring to a boil. Lower the heat to a simmer, cover, and cook until the peas break up, about 1 hour. If the soup seems too thick, you can add some more water or chicken broth. Taste to see if salt and pepper are to your liking. Remove the pot from the heat. Add the lemon juice, stir, and enjoy!

ROCKIN' *salads*

Colors Salad with Asian Honey-Lime Vinaigrette

Serves 4.

This salad practically screams healthy, and it's no slouch on taste. I love the colors, crunch, and touch of Asian flavor. It would go nicely with baked salmon and rice.

5 oz. Field greens, or about 4 big handfuls

1 small yellow pepper, diced

2 medium carrots, peeled and sliced

1 medium avocado, chopped

16 cherry tomatoes, cut in half

2 kiwis, peeled and chopped (can see HELPING HAND)

3 Tbsp. pumpkin seeds

For the vinaigrette:

2 Tbsp. olive oil

1 Tbsp. rice vinegar

1 tsp. Dijon mustard

2 tsp. honey

½ tsp. sesame oil

2 Tbsp. fresh lime juice

2 pinches Kosher salt

1/4 tsp. pepper

Whisk the vinaigrette ingredients together in a small bowl until well mixed and set aside. Wash and then dry the greens (a salad spinner makes an easy job of this). Transfer to a large salad bowl, along with the rest of the salad ingredients (except the pumpkin seeds). Toss with the vinaigrette, sprinkle with pumpkin seeds, and enjoy!

Quinoa Salad with
Red Onions, Pecans, Goat Cheese, and Avocado

....

Serves 4.

Quinoa is an uber-healthy grain that is native to South America. It has over 5,000 years of history, and unlike most grains, quinoa is a complete protein, meaning it contains all the essential amino acids in a balanced protein. I think you'll love its texture and satisfying nature. The sunflower seeds not only boast great flavor and crunch; they cater to your heart health with big doses of Vitamin C and E. You can use leftover quinoa just as you would rice.

1 large red onion, sliced

1/2 Tbsp. olive oil

½ tsp. Kosher salt

¼ tsp. pepper

1 cup quinoa

2 cups vegetable stock or water

1/3 cup pecans, chopped (can see HELPING HAND)

1 large avocado, chopped

2 oz. goat cheese, crumbled

For the dressing:

2 Tbsp. olive oil

1 Tbsp. red wine vinegar

1 tsp. Dijon mustard

1/8 tsp. salt

1/8 tsp. pepper

Preheat the oven to 400 degrees. Spray a rimmed baking sheet with Pam.

Place the red onion slices on the prepared baking sheet. Add the olive oil, salt and pepper. Toss together with your fingers. Cook for 18-20 minutes, until lightly golden, tossing once. Set aside.

Place the quinoa in a medium saucepan with 2 cups of water or stock. Stir and bring to a boil. Reduce the heat and simmer, covered, until the liquid is absorbed, about 10-15 minutes. When quinoa is done, the grains will be translucent and the outer layer of the grain will have popped off. Meanwhile, whisk all of the dressing ingredients together in a small bowl.

Prep the pecans and avocado, and get the goat cheese out. In a large bowl, combine the quinoa, red onion, pecans, and dressing. Add the avocado and goat cheese. Stir gently to combine.

Enjoy!

Spinach, Roasted Beets, Mushroom, and Sunflower Seed Salad with Citrus Vinaigrette

....

Serves 4.

You may not remember Popeye (but you can Google him). He was unstoppable, buoyed by his spinach intake! And, beets are not only a really cool red- fuchsia color; they are rich in antioxidants and support detoxification. Spinach and beets are nutritionally superior buddies that hang well together. Popeye would have loved this salad!

Plan ahead since the beets take about 45 minutes to cook. I like to save the beet greens and use them just like lettuce in sandwiches.

3 golf-ball sized beets, scrubbed, with stems and roots trimmed (can see HELPING HAND for Selecting and Preparing)

5 oz. baby spinach leaves, or 4 big handfuls

4 white button mushrooms, wiped clean (bottom of stems sliced off and discarded), and thinly sliced

¼ cup sunflower seeds

Optional: Some sliced fennel would be great in this salad too (can see HELPING HAND for Selecting and Preparing)

For the dressing (you'll have some left over):

2 Tbsp. fresh orange juice (can just squeeze an orange if you don't want to buy o.j.)

2 Tbsp. fresh lemon juice

1 tsp. honey

¼ tsp. Kosher salt

¼ tsp. pepper

Pinch of cayenne pepper

4 Tbsp. olive oil

Preheat the oven to 400 degrees.

Have a baking sheet on hand and ready to go.
Wrap the beets in foil. Place on a baking sheet and cook for about 45 minutes, until tender (easily pierced with a fork). If your beets are bigger than about golf ball size, it will take longer.

Place the dressing ingredients, except the olive oil, in a small bowl. Whisk to combine. Then, whisk in the olive oil until well mixed. Set aside.

When the beets are done and cool enough to handle, the skins should peel off rather easily. Rub the skin off with a paper towel so your hands don't get too pink. If you end up needing to use a knife, as soon as you are done, rinse any pinkness off your hands with soap and water (or a little lemon juice).

Cut the beets into eighths. Place them in your salad bowl. Wash and dry the spinach (a salad spinner makes an easy job of this). Add the spinach, mushrooms, pecans, and the vinaigrette to the beets.

Give the salad a toss and enjoy!

Pear Crouton, Gruyere and Cashew Salad with Maple Champagne Vinaigrette

....

Serves 4.

Inspired by a salad that I had at a favorite restaurant in Oregon, this one is kind of like a fruit and cheese snack, but in a salad! The maple syrup and champagne vinegar in the dressing give it just the right twist.

½ Tbsp. butter

1 medium (hard-not soft and ripe) Anjou pear (this is a green pear, as opposed to the golden brownish ones, which are Bosc pears), cut into "crouton" cubes-you may just want to eat the tips since they are less square!

¼ tsp. sugar

4 big handfuls of baby romaine lettuce

1/3 cup Gruyere cheese, cut into ½ inch cubes (about 1/8 lb.)

1/4 cup chopped unsalted cashews (can see HELPING HAND for how to chop)

Maple Champagne Vinaigrette:

2 Tbsp. olive oil

1 Tbsp. plus 1 tsp. champagne vinegar

½ tsp. Dijon mustard

1 small clove garlic, minced

1 1/2 tsp. pure maple syrup

1/8 tsp. Kosher salt

¼ tsp. pepper

Melt the butter in a medium skillet over medium heat. Swirl the pan to coat. Add the pear cubes in a single layer. Add the sugar. Cook for 4-6 minutes, tossing occasionally with tongs, until you have golden "croutons."

Meanwhile, make the vinaigrette by whisking all the ingredients together in a small bowl.

Wash, and then dry the lettuce (a salad spinner makes an easy job of this). Transfer to a large salad bowl, along with the Gruyere and cashews. Toss with the vinaigrette, top with "croutons," and enjoy!

Baby Arugula, Fig, and Pecorino Salad with Pine Nuts

....

Serves 4.

This salad seems like a flavor party! I guess there is a lot happening here: peppery arugula, with sweet fig, nutty Pecorino, and the buttery crunch of pine nuts. As for the leftover Pecorino, I like to use it in pastas and other dishes where you might normally use parmesan cheese.

4 big handfuls of baby arugula

2 Tbsp. olive oil

1 Tbsp. fresh lemon juice

A pinch of Kosher salt

Pepper, to taste

5 fresh figs, sliced *

About 1 oz. Pecorino cheese, shaved with your vegetable peeler

2 1/2 Tbsp. pine nuts, toasted (can see HELPING HAND for how to toast)

* Note that if fresh figs aren't in season, nectarines would be great in here. 1 medium size nectarine, thinly sliced, should do it.

Wash and then dry the arugula (a salad spinner makes an easy job of this). Transfer to a salad bowl and drizzle with olive oil and lemon juice. Add salt and pepper. Toss to combine. Add the figs and cheese and toss gently. Sprinkle with pine nuts.

Enjoy!

The Cobb Salad

....

Serves 4.

This salad is one of my husband's top favorites. I am often pressed for time, so I buy the pre-grilled chicken breasts from the prepared foods section of the store, and start from there. If you would prefer, either grill the chicken yourself, or follow the instructions in the HELPING HAND section for making plain sautéed chicken breasts. Toss the salad with my delicious champagne vinaigrette and enjoy!

1 large head of Romaine lettuce

3 store-bought plain grilled chicken breasts, chopped

1 medium avocado, chopped

4 eggs, hard boiled, chopped (can see HELPING HAND)

1/2 cup crumbled bleu cheese (2 ¾ oz.)

16 cherry tomatoes, cut into fourths (halved if small)

Champagne Vinaigrette:

1 garlic clove, minced

1/2 tsp. Dijon mustard

1/4 tsp. Kosher salt

¼ tsp. pepper

3 Tbsp. champagne vinegar

¼ cup olive oil, plus 2 Tbsp.

For the dressing:

Put the garlic, mustard, salt, pepper, and vinegar in a small bowl. Whisk to combine. Add the olive oil while whisking (putting the bowl on a damp towel helps the bowl stay put while you whisk), and mix until well combined. Set aside.

Remove any unsightly outer lettuce leaves. Cut the end off of the lettuce head, wash the leaves, and then dry them (a salad spinner makes an easy job of this). Lay the leaves on top of each other and slice the lettuce crosswise into thin ribbons, and then once lengthwise (so the ribbons aren't so long) OR just chop or tear with your hands. Put the lettuce in a large salad bowl.

On a plastic cutting sheet or a cutting board, slice the chicken breasts lengthwise into thin strips and then crosswise into more or less bite size pieces. Add the chicken and the remaining salad ingredients to the salad bowl, toss with the vinaigrette and enjoy!

Lentil Salad with Indian Spiced Olive Oil-Lemon Vinaigrette

Serves 4.

I brought this salad to a party and one of the guests searched me out to say how much he enjoyed it - and ask me how to make it. Of course that gave me a happy feeling! I knew this salad was a keeper.

Lentils are high in fiber, an inexpensive source of protein, and have a comforting, nutty flavor. French green lentils have a distinctive taste and should be pretty easy to find. If you have trouble, you can use regular brown lentils (just cook them for a bit less time).

1 cup French green lentils

3 cups chicken stock, vegetable stock, or water

3 garlic cloves, peeled and lightly crushed (can use the flat side of your chef's knife to give them a whack)

1 1/3 cups halved cherry tomatoes (quartered if they are large)

2 scallions, diced small

1 medium carrot, diced small

2 Tbsp. chopped fresh basil

2 Tbsp. chopped fresh parsley

For the dressing:

2 Tbsp. olive oil

2 Tbsp. fresh lemon juice

½ tsp. garlic powder

1 tsp. curry powder

½ tsp. coriander

½ tsp. dry mustard

¼ tsp. Kosher salt

¼ tsp. pepper

Sort through the lentils to make sure there are no small stones or bits that shouldn't be there - you can just spread them out on a clean (white or light colored) kitchen towel to do the sorting. Rinse the lentils in a colander under cool water.

Pour the stock or water into a medium saucepan, and add the lentils and garlic. Stir and bring to a boil. Lower the heat to a simmer and cook, uncovered, for about 14 minutes, (until just tender, but not mushy).

Meanwhile, whisk the dressing ingredients together in a small bowl and set aside.

Prep your tomatoes, scallions, carrots, basil, and parsley.

Drain the lentils and transfer to your serving bowl. Remove the garlic (and discard). Add the tomatoes, scallions, carrots, basil, and parsley to the bowl and gently toss with the lentils. Drizzle the dressing over the veggie mixture, gently toss, and serve.

Spinach Salad with
Blueberries, Strawberries, Walnuts, and Bleu Cheese

Serves 4.

Inspired by a salad I enjoyed in Boston, this salad combines sweet, crunch, and tang. I also love that three antioxidant powerhouses- spinach and the berries- share center stage. It's fast to prepare and good-looking, too! If you enjoy goat cheese, it would make an excellent substitute for the bleu cheese in this salad.

For the vinaigrette:

½ medium shallot, minced (1 Tbsp.)

1 Tbsp. sherry vinegar (I like "Vinagre de Jerez")

pinch of Kosher salt

2 pinches pepper

4 Tbsp. olive oil

About 5 oz. baby spinach leaves, or 4 big handfuls

½ cup blueberries, rinsed and dried*

½ cup sliced strawberries

2 oz. crumbled bleu cheese

1/3 cup chopped walnuts

Put the shallot, vinegar, salt and pepper in a small bowl, stir to combine, and let sit for 5 minutes. Whisk the olive oil in until well mixed. Set aside.

Wash and then dry the spinach (a salad spinner makes an easy job of this). Place the salad ingredients in a large bowl, toss with some of the vinaigrette, and enjoy.

* My technique for the blueberries: rinse them and place on a clean kitchen towel. If the towel is big enough, use the sides and gently roll over the berries. If not, take a paper towel and gently roll over the berries.

Best Caesar Salad

Serves 4-6.

Caesar salad is my very favorite salad. At restaurants, my family has gotten used to my server quiz: "Is the dressing classic--made with olive oil, lemon juice, and anchovies? Or is it creamy?" As you can probably guess, I don't favor "creamy" and am suspicious of the ingredients! Anyway, mine is really quick to prepare once you have done it a few times. And, if you're a fan like me, there's nothing like having the best Caesar at your fingertips whenever you want.

1 large head of Romaine lettuce

3 anchovies, chopped

1/8 tsp. salt

2 large garlic cloves, roughly chopped (just makes it easier to make the paste)

1 Tbsp. fresh lemon juice

1 tsp. sherry vinegar (I like La Posada, from Spain)*

½ tsp. Dijon mustard

1 tsp. Worcestershire sauce

1/4 tsp. pepper

¼ cup olive oil

1/3 cup grated parmesan cheese

If you are a crouton fan, or want to impress your friends, see the recipe for Homemade Croutons below.

For the homemade croutons:

The bread I like best for these is Ciabatta. Others, like a baguette or sourdough, would work also.

3 cups Ciabatta bread, cut into medium crouton cubes

1 Tbsp. Olive oil

1/2 Tbsp. butter, melted

Scant sprinkling of cayenne pepper (gives the croutons a nice "bite")

Preheat the oven to 450 degrees.

Have a cookie sheet ready to use.

Mix the olive oil and butter in a medium bowl. Add the bread cubes and toss so that the bread cubes are coated (I use my fingers!). Sprinkle a bit of cayenne pepper over the bread and toss again. Put the croutons in a single layer on the cookie sheet and bake until golden, about 6 minutes. Voila!

For the salad:

Remove any unsightly outer lettuce leaves. Cut the end off, wash, and then dry the lettuce with your salad spinner. Chop or tear and put into a large salad bowl.

To make the dressing, on your plastic cutting sheet or a cutting board, make a paste out of the anchovies, salt and garlic by mashing down on them with a fork. When this is done, scrape the paste off of the cutting sheet/board with the fork, and place in a small bowl. Add the lemon juice, vinegar, mustard, Worcestershire sauce, and pepper and whisk to combine.

Add the olive oil while whisking (putting the bowl on a damp towel helps the bowl stay put while you whisk) and mix until well combined.

Pour the dressing over the lettuce, add the parmesan cheese (and croutons, if using), and toss.

* Note: you can substitute red wine vinegar if necessary, but if you buy the sherry vinegar, it will last a really long time. If you love Caesar salad, buy the sherry!

Raw Kale and Sweet Leaf Lettuce Salad

....

Serves 6.

This salad is the epitome of refreshing! I love the "meaty" kale contrasted with the sweet leaf lettuces, both chopped small. The robust red wine vinaigrette and crunchy squash, cukes, and carrots make it a pleasure to enjoy. This would be great as a side with a pasta dish.

1 medium-large bunch kale, leaves chopped very small

2 big handfuls sweet leaf spring mix lettuces, chopped small

2 small carrots, diced small

1 medium yellow squash, diced small

½ medium English cucumber, diced small

A couple handfuls grape tomatoes

2 tbsp. shaved (or grated) parmesan cheese

For the Red Wine Vinaigrette:

3 Tbsp. red wine vinegar

¼ tsp. ground mustard

1 tsp. whole grain mustard

¼ tsp. garlic powder

¼ tsp. pepper

¼ tsp. Kosher salt

1 tsp. capers

½ small shallot, minced

6 Tbsp. olive oil

Combine all the dressing ingredients, except the olive oil, in a small bowl. Whisk the olive oil in and mix well.

Wash the kale and give it a few good shakes over the sink. Remove the hard spines by folding the kale lengthwise and cutting the spine out with a knife. Discard the spines and chop the kale leaves. Prepare the rest of the salad ingredients and add to your salad bowl as you go. Follow the directions for Red Wine Vinaigrette and add about ¼ cup of dressing (or to your taste). Toss the salad and enjoy!

Raw Beet Salad with Pistachio Nibs

....

Serves 2-4.

Some folks think of beets as peasant food or old fashioned, maybe due in part to the canned variety, where beets rest in watery magenta colored juice until released. Fresh beets put on a whole different show!

A food processor makes super quick work of this salad (hand grating will do as well)*. The slight citrus with a touch of sweet and mint are a perfect foil for the pistachio crunch.

3 small-medium beets

2 Tbsp. chopped mint

1 Tbsp. honey

1 Tbsp. fresh lemon juice

1 Tbsp. olive oil

¼ tsp. Kosher salt

1/8 cup pistachio nuts, chopped a bit (can see HELPING HAND)

Wash/scrub the beets really well. Dry them. Cut off the ends, making sure to cut off any part that might have dirt attached. Chop the beets into pieces that will fit in the feeder tube of your food processor. Use the grater attachment and grate. Place the beets in a medium bowl. Add the remaining ingredients, stir to combine, and enjoy!

* If you grate the beets by hand, your skin will take on the beet color. So, either wear gloves or rinse your hands right away. If you need more help, use lemon juice, and rub your hands with table salt. That should do the trick!

Summer Quinoa Salad with
Tomatoes, Fresh Basil, and Fresh Mozzarella

....

Serves 4-6.

A wonderful summertime salad, the quinoa offers a superb protein component to complement the light, snappy dressing and fresh vegetables. Almost any type of white fish, such as halibut, snapper, tilapia, or sea bass would be delicious served right on the top of the salad.*

1 ½ cups quinoa

3 cups vegetable stock or water

3 Tbsp. red wine vinegar

6 Tbsp. olive oil

1 large clove garlic, minced

½ small shallot, minced

3/4 tsp. Dijon mustard

3/4 tsp. dried oregano

3/4 tsp. Kosher salt

¼ tsp. pepper

Small container cherry tomatoes, halved

1/3 cup yellow bell peppers, chopped

1 medium zucchini, chopped into small cubes (about 1 cup)

1/2 cup basil leaves, packed down, roughly chopped

½ lb. fresh mozzarella cheese, cut into small cubes

3 cups baby arugula or baby spinach, packed down, chopped

Place the quinoa in a medium saucepan with 3 cups of stock or water. Stir and bring to a boil. Reduce the heat and simmer, covered, until the liquid is absorbed, about 10 - 15 minutes. When the quinoa is done, the grains will be translucent and the outer layer of the grain will have popped off.

Meanwhile, whisk the red wine vinegar, olive oil, garlic, shallot, mustard, oregano, salt, and pepper together in a small bowl and set aside.

Prep the tomatoes, bell pepper, zucchini, basil, mozzarella cheese, and arugula or spinach.

Put the cooked quinoa in a large bowl and spread out to cool (10 minutes should do it).

Fluff the quinoa with a fork, and add the tomatoes, bell peppers, zucchini, basil, mozzarella cheese, arugula or spinach, and dressing. Gently toss to combine.

*To prepare the fish (I suggest about 6 oz. per person), if using: drizzle with about 1 Tbsp. of olive oil and sprinkle with Kosher salt and pepper to taste. Bake in a 400 degree oven for 16-18 minutes, until cooked through. To test, slice through the thickest part. It should not look raw, will have milky white juices, and flake easily.

QUICK + TASTY
salad dressings

Note that when whisking olive oil into other dressing ingredients,
you can place a damp kitchen towel under the bowl to help it stay put.

Also, extra dressing will keep in the fridge.

Bleu Cheese Vinaigrette

2 Tbsp. red wine vinegar
2 Tbsp. water
¼ tsp. garlic powder
¼ tsp. onion powder
½ tsp. Kosher salt
¼ tsp. pepper
1 medium clove garlic, minced
½ tsp. Dijon mustard
¼ cup olive oil
½ cup crumbled blue cheese

Place the red wine vinegar, water, spices, garlic, and mustard in a small bowl. Whisk to combine. Whisk the olive oil in and mix well. Add the bleu cheese and stir to combine.

Champagne Vinaigrette

3 Tbsp. champagne vinegar
2 garlic cloves, minced
1/2 tsp. Dijon mustard
1/4 tsp. Kosher salt
¼ tsp. pepper
¼ cup olive oil, plus 2 Tbsp.

Combine the vinegar, garlic, mustard, salt, and pepper in a small bowl. Whisk the olive oil in and mix well.

Citrus Vinaigrette

2 Tbsp. fresh orange juice (can just squeeze an orange if you don't want to buy o.j.)
2 Tbsp. fresh lemon juice
1 tsp. honey
¼ tsp. Kosher salt
¼ tsp. pepper
Pinch of cayenne pepper
4 Tbsp. olive oil

Combine the orange juice, lemon juice, honey, salt, pepper, and cayenne pepper. Whisk the olive oil in and mix well.

Lemon and Olive Oil Dressing

2 Tbsp. fresh lemon juice
4 Tbsp. olive oil
Pinch of Kosher or sea salt
Pepper to taste

Whisk the lemon juice and olive oil together. Sprinkle the salad with salt and pepper and dress.

Red Wine Vinaigrette

3 Tbsp. red wine vinegar
¼ tsp. ground mustard
1 tsp. whole grain mustard
¼ tsp. garlic powder
¼ tsp. pepper
¼ tsp. Kosher salt
1 tsp. capers
½ small shallot, minced
6 Tbsp. olive oil

Combine all the ingredients, except the olive oil, in a small bowl. Whisk the olive oil in and mix well.

Sherry Vinaigrette

1 medium shallot, diced
2 Tbsp. sherry vinegar (I like "Vinagre De Jerez")
Healthy pinch of Kosher salt
1/8 tsp. pepper
8 Tbsp. olive oil

Place the shallot in a small bowl with the vinegar, salt, and pepper. Let it sit for about 5 minutes. Whisk in the olive oil until well combined.

After a good dinner, one can forgive anybody, even one's own relatives.

- Oscar Wilde

MAIN *eats*

No Fry Eggplant Parmesan

....

Serves 6.

Eggplant Parmesan is definitely one of my favorite dishes. Traditionally, the eggplant slices are breaded and fried. But, since a frying slice of eggplant drinks oil like a thirsty explorer, I wanted a different way. Broiling works really well, and I think the resulting dish is actually much fresher tasting.

3 medium eggplants, peeled and sliced into rounds about ¼ to ½ inch thick (can see HELPING HAND)

6 Tbsp. olive oil (about 2 per eggplant)

2/3 cup grated parmesan cheese, plus 3 Tbsp. for topping the finished dish

2/3 cup grated "low moisture part skim" mozzarella cheese

1 jar store bought marinara sauce-about 25 oz. (choose one with few ingredients, starting with tomatoes, no corn syrup, and little, if any, sugar).

Set oven to broil and place the oven rack under the broiler.

Spray a cookie sheet with Pam and have a pastry brush ready to use.

Place the eggplant slices on the cookie sheet and the olive oil in a little container. Brush each slice with just a bit of olive oil. Flip over and repeat. Place in the oven and cook until golden on top. It doesn't take long! Maybe 4-6 minutes. Sometimes, after 4 minutes, I rotate the pan if it looks like the slices aren't browning evenly.

Take the pan out, flip the eggplant slices and sprinkle each slice with a pinch of parmesan cheese. Broil again until golden. Repeat this process until all the eggplant is cooked.

Preheat the oven to 375 degrees.

Pour enough marinara sauce to coat the bottom of a baking dish (8x8 works nicely, but no need to be really exact). Top with a layer of slightly overlapping eggplant slices (cover up the sauce).

Sprinkle with about a third of the parmesan cheese and mozzarella cheese. Spoon some marinara sauce over the top, about ½ cup.

Repeat twice with a layer of eggplant, parmesan cheese, mozzarella cheese and sauce. If you have extra eggplant for the top layer, that's fine- use it! Note that I use a little more sauce for the top layer than the others, about ¾ cup. Sprinkle with 3 Tbsp. parmesan cheese.

Bake until the dish is bubbling a little around the edges (about 20 minutes). You just want it to be hot all the way through. Enjoy!

Note: If you prefer eggplant parmesan that is less sauce-y, just add less when you do your layering.

Homemade Pizza with 5 Star Sauce

....

Makes 1 large pizza.

Pizza is one of my very favorite foods. I've always thought of pizza as pretty wholesome, but of course it's even more so when you make it yourself. One of my recipe testers was fairly intimidated by the prospect of making this, but found it so tasty and do-able that she made it again a couple of weeks later (she and her husband raved about the sauce). Poetry to my ears!

Plan ahead a bit since the dough rests for 40 minutes.

½ cup plus 3 Tbsp. warm water (I like to test the temperature by running it over the inside of my wrist. If the water is pretty warm, not hot, it is good.)

1 tsp. sugar

1 packet active dry yeast

2 cups flour

2 tsp. Canola oil (plus an extra tsp. for oiling the bowl)

1 16 oz. jar store bought pizza sauce (buy one with few ingredients, starting with tomatoes, no corn syrup and little, if any, sugar). You'll have some leftover sauce (maybe pasta later in the week?). Or, try my easy, quick, homemade pizza sauce recipe on the next page (you'll love it!)

1 cup grated "low moisture-part skim" mozzarella cheese

½ cup grated parmesan cheese

Optional: other toppings, like mushrooms, olives, fresh baby spinach, sun dried tomatoes, peppers, onions, jalapenos, or fresh tomatoes. Naturally, this recipe stays healthier if you don't add processed/high fat meats as a topping.

Add 1 tsp. sugar to the warm water in the measuring cup.

Stir to dissolve the sugar. Sprinkle the yeast packet over the top and let sit for 10 minutes. It will become foamy.

Meanwhile, measure the flour into a medium size bowl.

Add the yeast mixture and 2 tsp. oil to the flour. Combine with a wooden spoon to get it somewhat mixed. Then, with clean hands, mix the rest of the way. Turn the dough out onto a clean, lightly floured work area. Knead (this means you push forward on the ball of dough with the heels of your hands, fold the dough over itself from the right, then the left, and repeat) about 25 times, until smooth.

Rinse and dry the medium bowl you just used, add 1 tsp. of oil, and coat the bowl. Turn the ball of dough in the bowl to coat with the oil.

Cover the bowl with a damp towel and let the dough sit for about 40 minutes, in a draft free place.

Preheat oven to 425 degrees. Sprinkle 1 Tbsp. cornmeal on a large pizza pan or cookie sheet that has been sprayed with Pam.

Start to shape the dough by flattening it out, first while you are holding it, then onto your prepared pan. Just keep pressing it outward and flattening it to more or less the size of your pan - not too thick and not too thin (you want it to "support" your toppings).

Top with pizza sauce (spreading with the back of a spoon works well) and the cheeses. Use an amount of sauce that you like. Add any other favorite toppings. Bake the pizza until golden on the bottom and the cheese is melted, about 17 minutes.

Homemade Pizza Sauce

....

1 Tbsp. olive oil

2 cloves of garlic, sliced thin

1 (28 oz.) can crushed tomatoes (I like Cento and San Marzano)

1 heaping Tbsp. tomato paste

¼ tsp. garlic powder

1 tsp. honey

½ tsp. Kosher salt

¼ tsp. dried oregano

¼ tsp. pepper

Heat the oil in a medium saucepan over low heat. Add the garlic, and cook, stirring, until fragrant, about 1 minute. Add the remaining ingredients and stir. Increase heat to medium-low. Simmer for 5 minutes and you are ready to go! If the sauce splatters too much, reduce the heat or cover part way.

The Spaghetti and Marinara Sauce

....

Serves 4-6.

This marinara has gotten rave reviews. It's pure, simple, quick, and delicious! It starts with one of the best cooking aromas- garlic being sautéed in olive oil. Then, with the fresh basil and some good tomatoes, you can't go wrong.

*If **Pasta with Sun Dried Tomatoes and Goat Cheese** sounds good to you (sometimes I'll use angel hair pasta for this), sprinkle the pasta and marinara with 8 oz. chopped (packed in olive oil) sundried tomatoes, and toss. Then, sprinkle with about 3 oz. crumbled goat cheese and a little chopped parsley, and serve. If you're a mushroom fan, you can also sauté about 8 oz. sliced mushrooms in 1 Tbsp. olive oil while the sauce cooks and add those when you add the sun dried tomatoes. Yum!*

12 oz. of spaghetti (whole wheat if you choose)

3 Tbsp. olive oil

5 good sized cloves garlic, minced

1/2 tsp. crushed red pepper flakes (less if you like less heat)

3/4 tsp. Kosher salt

28 oz. can crushed tomatoes (try to use an organic one)

3 Tbsp. fresh basil, chopped

Garnish: 2 Tbsp. parmesan cheese, optional

Heat a large pot of water (about ¾ full) to boiling.

Heat the olive oil in a large skillet over medium heat. Add the garlic, red pepper flakes, and salt and cook for 2 minutes, while stirring. You want the garlic to be "sizzling", but don't let it brown (light golden is o.k.). Add the tomatoes and stir to combine. Bring to a slow boil (simmer). Cover and simmer for 15 minutes. Remove the pot from the heat and stir in the chopped basil.

When the pasta water comes to a boil, add 1 tsp. of salt and the pasta. Give it a stir. Follow the package directions for cooking time. You want the pasta to end up "al dente." This means a little bit firm, but not hard in the middle. Carefully lift a strand out of the water with a fork, try it, and see. Drain the pasta in a colander.

Pour the drained pasta into the sauce and toss with your tongs. Use an exaggerated movement, lifting the pasta as you mix (this introduces some air into the process, making the dish come together very nicely). Continue until the sauce is fully incorporated. Feel the artist in you-it's fun!

Sprinkle with parmesan cheese, if using.

Baked Ziti with Sausage-Spiced Turkey, Pumpkin, and Kale

....

Serves 6.

Baked ziti is an awesome comfort dish. In mine, the subtly spiced pumpkin and the turkey "sausage" are a super taste match. And, I like the kale addition for its flavor and for the respectable health boost that it gives this dish! Oh, and you can freeze the extra sage for a later use.

12 oz. ziti

For the turkey:

1 lb. ground turkey (1/2 thighs, ½ breast)

1 Tbsp. chopped fresh sage

½ tsp. garlic powder

¼ tsp. oregano

1/4 tsp. salt

½ tsp. pepper

For the pumpkin mix:

15 oz. can 100% pure pumpkin

1/8 tsp. allspice

Pinch cinnamon

1/8 tsp. ground ginger

14 oz. can fat free evaporated milk

For the cheese combination:

1 cup 2% cottage cheese

1 cup part-skim ricotta cheese

1/4 cup grated pecorino romano cheese

For the kale layer:

3 cups (packed down) kale, roughly chopped*

¼ tsp. salt

For the topping:

1/2 cup grated part-skim mozzarella cheese

1/4 cup grated pecorino romano cheese

Note regarding kale: After washing, give the leaves a good couple of shakes over the sink to remove most of the water. Also, before you chop the leaves, cut the hard spine away from each leaf and discard. For info on selecting kale, can see HELPING HAND.

Bring a large pot of water to a boil.
Prep the kale and chop the sage.
Preheat oven to 425 degrees. Spray a 9x13 glass baking dish with Pam.

Cook the turkey in a large skillet over medium heat, stirring occasionally, until no longer pink (about 7 minutes). Drain any fat by holding the top of the pan over the turkey and tilting the pan over the sink. Add the sage and spices, and then stir until fragrant and combined, about 1 minute. Remove turkey from the skillet and set aside.

When the pasta water boils, add a tsp. of salt and the pasta. Stir, and cook for about 8 minutes. It's o.k. if the pasta isn't fully cooked, as it will cook more in the oven. Remove the pot from the heat, drain the pasta and return the pasta to the pot.

In the same skillet you cooked the turkey in, over medium-low heat, combine pumpkin and spices with a whisk. Add the milk gradually and cook, whisking occasionally, until heated through, about 2 minutes.

Add the pumpkin mixture and turkey to the pasta and stir. Make the cheese combination by mixing the cottage cheese, ricotta cheese, and ¼ cup pecorino in a medium bowl until combined.

Place half the pasta in your baking dish. Spread half the cheese combination over the pasta (I like to dollop pretty evenly, and then spread with the back of a spoon). Top with the chopped kale. Sprinkle evenly with ¼ tsp. salt. Add the other half of the pasta, and the other half of the cheese mix. Top with ¼ cup of pecorino and the mozzarella cheese. Spray the inside of a piece of foil with Pam so the cheese won't stick, and cook, covered for about 20 minutes. It should be hot and bubbly. Enjoy!

Moist and Tasty Veggie Burgers

....

Makes 4.

Making homemade veggie burgers may sound like trouble, but really, this recipe is quite a breeze to prepare. I love the white beans, arugula, basil, and whole grain mustard flavors, combined with the almond crunch. Even if you don't normally like veggie burgers, give these a try. You might be surprised!

You can make these a couple of hours ahead and keep in the fridge until you are ready to cook. If you can, take them out a bit before to take some of the chill out. Pick up the burgers gently with both hands and place in your pan.

15 oz. can Cannellini beans (with few added ingredients), rinsed and drained

4 medium Cremini mushrooms, wiped clean, bottom of stems removed (and discarded), and diced

1/4 small onion, minced

1 stalk celery, diced

3 garlic cloves, minced

1 ½ tsp. whole grain mustard

2 cups loosely packed baby arugula, chopped

1/3 cup sliced almonds, chopped (can see HELPING HAND)

¼ cup fresh basil (packed down), chopped

1 tsp. Worcestershire sauce

1/2 tsp. Kosher salt

1/8 tsp. cayenne pepper

1 Tbsp. olive oil

On your cutting board or plastic cutting sheet (I prefer these), mash the beans with a fork. Place the beans in a medium bowl. Add the remaining ingredients, except for the olive oil, and stir with a large spoon to combine.

After they are well mixed, kind of flatten the mix while in the bowl and "score" it with a knife so you can visualize 4 more or less equal size patties. Heat a large skillet over medium heat and add the olive oil. Swirl the pan to coat with oil. Form the veggie mixture into patties and place in the skillet.

Cook until golden on one side, about 7-9 minutes. Flip and cook for about 6 minutes on the other side, until golden. Don't worry if they don't flip perfectly; just smush the edges back together with your spatula. Voila!

Hearty Mushroom and Sausage Lasagna

Serves 6.

Here is a hearty and satisfying variation of lasagna that is sure to please. The sausage and mushrooms are a natural flavor match, and the no cook noodles make this recipe easier than many. Plan ahead a bit since the lasagna takes 45 minutes to bake.

1 lb. package no cook lasagna noodles (you'll have some left over)

1 Tbsp. olive oil

8 oz. package of mushrooms, wiped clean, stem bottoms sliced off (discard), and sliced

4 garlic cloves, minced

3/4 lb. Italian chicken sausage*

3/4 lb. Italian spicy beef sausage*

26 oz. jar marinara sauce (choose one with few ingredients, starting with tomatoes, no corn syrup, and little, if any, sugar).

1 ½ cups 2% cottage cheese

8 oz. grated "low moisture-part skim" mozzarella cheese

6 Tbsp. Parmesan cheese, plus 2 Tbsp. for topping the finished dish

Note regarding the sausages: Many higher quality stores carry these fresh sausages in their meat department. Just slice the casing and remove the meat.

Preheat the oven to 375 degrees.

Heat a large skillet over medium heat. Add 1 Tbsp. olive oil and swirl the pan to coat. Add the mushrooms, and spread out in one layer. Turn the heat to medium high. Let the mushrooms cook until they are turning golden, about 5 minutes. Lower the heat to medium. Add the garlic, and cook 1 minute more, while stirring. Add the sausage. Stir, while breaking the sausage up with the back of a wooden spoon. Cook until the sausage is no longer pink, about 10 minutes, stirring occasionally. Set aside.

Pour ¾ cup marinara sauce in the bottom of your pan to coat.

Now, proceed to layer as follows:

About 4 noodles, or enough to cover the bottom of the pan. If you need to customize a noodle size by breaking it, go right ahead!

1/2 cup cottage cheese (spread out with the back of a spoon)

½ cup mozzarella cheese

2 Tbsp. Parmesan cheese

1/3 of the sausage mixture (I don't use the liquid at the bottom of the pan)

1/3 cup sauce

Repeat 2 more times.

Pour 1 1/3 cups of marinara over the top, and in the corners.

Spread with a spoon. Distribute ½ cup mozzarella cheese and 2 Tbsp. parmesan cheese over the top.

Cover tightly with foil (spray the inside of the foil lightly with Pam so the cheese doesn't stick).

Cook for 45 minutes.

Note: Leftovers are best heated in the oven (300 degrees), rather than in the microwave.

So Fresh Tasting Chicken Parmesan

Serves 4.

Chicken parmesan is an Italian favorite and our son, Benjy, says mine is the best. Trust me, he's honest with his opinions! The chicken in my recipe is not breaded and fried as the classic normally is; I think that makes the flavors of the dish come through extra loud and clear.

1 Tbsp. olive oil

4 boneless, skinless chicken breasts, (if they are pretty fat,

I like to slice them in half, horizontally--makes them cook faster, and stay moist)*

1/2 tsp. Kosher salt, divided

¼ tsp. pepper, divided

1 ½ cups store bought marinara sauce (buy one with few ingredients , starting with tomatoes, no corn syrup and little, if any, sugar)

1/3 cup grated parmesan cheese, plus 2 Tbsp. for sprinkling over the finished dish

2/3 cup shredded mozzarella cheese

Preheat oven to 350 degrees.
Have a glass baking dish (9x13 works well) ready to use.

Prep the chicken (see HELPING HAND). Heat a large skillet over medium heat. Add the olive oil. Season the chicken breasts (one side) with 1/4 tsp. salt and 1/8 tsp. pepper. Swirl the pan to coat with oil. Put the breasts in the pan, seasoned side down. Season the top side of the breasts with the rest of the salt and pepper. Cook for 5-6 minutes on medium-high heat, or until golden. Then, flip the chicken and repeat. The chicken does not have to be cooked through because it will cook more in the oven.

Pour about 1/2 cup of the sauce in your baking dish. Add the chicken, in a single layer. Sprinkle with some parmesan cheese. Top with half the mozzarella. Spoon some marinara over each piece of chicken and repeat: some parmesan, mozzarella, and marinara. Top with a sprinkling of parmesan cheese. If you have extra, and like it sauce-y, pour more sauce between and around the chicken. Bake for about 15 minutes or until the cheese is melted and the sauce is bubbly. Enjoy!

* Here's how I do it - just be careful since raw chicken is slippery -

Place the chicken breast on a cutting sheet/board and find the thickest part of the breast. Place your hand on top of the breast, and very carefully, and slowly, use a good chef's knife and start slicing. As you get toward the middle, use the hand that was on top to separate the top from the bottom (open the chicken like a book), and slowly cut the rest of the way through.

Whole Roasted Lemon Chicken - 7 Easy Steps

Serves 4.

Roasted Chicken is a great idea for dinner when you want something wholesome and extremely easy to prepare. You just get it in the oven and forget about it for a while. Plan ahead a bit since it cooks for a couple of hours.

We like to eat this with some roasted veggies and a green salad.

1 whole chicken, free range , organic, if possible (4-5 lbs.)

1 tsp. olive oil

1/2 tsp. Kosher salt

1/4 tsp. pepper

1 lemon

Sometimes you will find extra parts- heart, liver, giblets- in a little bag (or not in a bag) in the chicken cavity, or at the other end. Just be sure to remove it. Cut off any extra fat/skin hanging off the chicken (e.g. near the opening or the other end of the cavity). Remove and discard any string that might be holding the raw chicken together.

1. Preheat the oven to 350 degrees and spray a roasting pan with Pam.

2. Have a piece of kitchen twine* (long enough to tie the drumsticks together) cut and ready to use.

3. Poke the lemon several times with a fork or the tip of a sharp paring knife, and give it a little squeeze.

4. Rinse the chicken inside and out, and pat dry with a paper towel, inside and out.

5. Place the lemon inside the chicken cavity.

6. Tie the drumsticks together. At this point, I like to tuck the tips of the chicken wings under the bird (lay the wing out flat and push each tip back under the bird-toward you).

7. Place the chicken in the pan. Drizzle the olive oil over the chicken and rub around; season with the salt and pepper, and rub around.

Cook for 2 hours. Test for doneness: the juices should run clear if you cut/pierce between the leg and the thigh.

Check the chicken after about an hour and a half. If it has become pretty brown, cover it lightly with a sheet of aluminum foil. This will prevent over-browning. Enjoy!

* Kitchen twine is string that won't burn if you put it in the oven. You can find it where you find other kitchen supplies.

No Tortilla Chicken Enchiladas

....

Serves 4.

This recipe was born while my husband was trying to cut down on carbs. He loves Mexican food, so when I thought about making enchiladas one night, I figured yes, but without the tortillas! No Tortilla Chicken Enchiladas has become a real favorite at our house. I like to serve it with fresh guacamole and some type of roasted vegetable.

1 ¾ lbs. chicken breasts, boneless and skinless

½ cup light sour cream

4 oz. reduced fat Monterrey jack cheese, grated, plus 2 Tbsp. for topping the finished dish

1 ½ cups enchilada sauce (try to buy one with pretty straightforward ingredients)

Optional garnishes: Salsa of choice, Guacamole

Preheat the oven to 350 degrees.

Spray a glass baking dish with Pam (8x8 works well).

Prep the chicken breasts (see HELPING HAND), but there is no need to pat them dry. Put the breasts into a large saucepan and add water to a little more than cover them. Bring to a boil, turn down the heat to a gentle boil (simmer) and let them cook, uncovered, for about 10 minutes (they will cook more in the oven). Place the breasts on your cutting board or plastic cutting sheet.

When they are cool enough to handle, chop into roughly bite size pieces and place in a large bowl (so it will be easy for you to mix in the other ingredients). Add the sour cream, cheese and enchilada sauce and stir to combine. Pour into the baking dish. Top with the extra cheese. Bake until it bubbles a little around the edges, about 15-20 minutes.

Enjoy!

Chicken and Sausage Jambalaya, Risotto Style

Serves 4 - 6.

Your tasty comfort meal in a pot has arrived! This Jambalaya, a Southern fave, begins with the traditional onions, celery, and garlic combo. The chicken and sausage work really well here with the tomatoes, hearty spices, and creamy textured rice. I like to top my dish off with a little hot sauce; then I'm good to go.

1 Tbsp. olive oil

1 medium onion, chopped

3 stalks celery, chopped

5 cloves garlic, minced

12 oz. turkey sausage* ("fully cooked"), cut into bite size pieces

28 oz. can diced tomatoes (with few added ingredients)

1 lb. chicken tenders, cut into roughly bite size pieces

1 cup long grain white rice (Uncle Ben's is best)

12 pimento stuffed green olives, roughly chopped

2 cups chicken broth (mostly fat free is pretty easy to find)

¾ tsp. garlic powder

½ tsp. onion powder

¼ tsp. turmeric

¼ tsp. cayenne pepper

¼ tsp. salt

Prep your onions and celery. Heat the oil in a large saucepan/soup pot over medium heat. Add the onions and celery and cook until softened, about 6 minutes, stirring occasionally. Meanwhile, prep your garlic and turkey sausage.

Add the garlic and cook for 1 minute, while stirring. Add the sausage and cook for about 4 minutes, stirring occasionally, to begin blending the flavors.

Add the tomatoes, and all of the remaining ingredients to the pot. Stir to combine, and bring to a boil. Reduce the heat to a simmer, cover, and cook until the liquid is absorbed, about 38 minutes. Stir 2-3 times while cooking.

Enjoy!

* Buy a good quality sausage, with few, pronounce-able ingredients. I usually make this recipe with turkey kielbasa sausage. Smoked turkey sausage would be great also.

Old World Tabeet

....

Serves 6.

Tabeet is one of my Mom's traditional Middle Eastern specialties. She has been making this delicious dish for as long as I can remember! A more understandable name, perhaps, would be "I-Cook-Myself Mediterranean Chicken and Rice," because it basically does! This is quintessential comfort food, but with magical flavors from distant places.

While the recipe is quick and easy to put together, the chicken does cook for a good portion of the day, so plan ahead for that.

1 whole chicken-3 to 4 lbs. (extra fat hanging around either end of the cavity removed), plus 2 chicken breasts and 2 legs

1 large onion, sliced

5 carrots, chopped into large chunks

5 stalks celery, chopped

2 cups long grain rice (Uncle Ben's is best)

5 cups water

1 medium tomato, chopped

3 Tbsp. Worcestershire sauce

2 Tbsp. Canola oil

4 oz. tomato paste

1 ¼ tsp. cinnamon

1 ¼ tsp. allspice

½ tsp. cloves

1 ¼ tsp. salt

1 tsp. pepper

Preheat the oven to 350 degrees.

Have these ready to go: a large roasting pan with a top and some kitchen twine to tie the drumsticks together.

Remove the extra parts from the whole chicken (liver, heart, giblets) that you'll sometimes find in the cavity or at the rear end. Discard the liver. Throw the heart and giblets into the roasting pan if you like them.

Rinse the chicken inside and out.

Tie the drumsticks together with the kitchen twine. Set aside. Place all the ingredients in the roasting pan. Stir to combine. Place the chicken in the pan, kind of wiggling it in among the other ingredients. Add the chicken pieces. Just kind of gently swirl the other ingredients around the chicken. You're set to go. Cover the pan and cook for 2 hours on 350. Then lower the heat to 250, and cook for another 3 ½ to 4 hours. If the chicken is getting pretty brown after 4 or 5 hours, just cover it lightly with a piece of foil (and put the top back on the pan).

Old Fashioned Brisket

....

Serves 6.

What a homey aroma fills the kitchen as this brisket cooks! Pair it with some rice (I love it with red rice) or roasted potatoes and a green vegetable, and you're poised for truly satisfying repast. Or, if you love potatoes flavored by the brisket, you can "throw" some fingerling potatoes (halved) into the mix when you add the other veggies to the roasting pan. They're called fingerlings because they look like little gnarly fingers!

While preparing this recipe is super easy, keep in mind that it takes hours to cook. So plan ahead!

4 lb. brisket (pick a pretty lean one, though they all have some fat on one side)

1 large onion, peeled and sliced

4 carrots, chopped

1/2 cup ketchup, plus 2 Tbsp.

5 Tbsp. Worcestershire sauce, plus 1 tsp.

1 Tbsp. brown sugar

1 ½ tsp. dry mustard powder

1 tsp. garlic powder

1 tsp. onion powder

¼ tsp. pepper

1 cup water

Preheat the oven to 300 degrees.

You'll need a roasting pan with a cover.

Rinse the brisket and pat dry with a paper towel. Place in the roasting pan, fat side up. Scatter the onions and carrots around the brisket. Top the brisket with the remaining ingredients (except the water) and spread over the top and around the sides of the brisket with the back of a spoon. Pour the water around the outside of the brisket. Give the pan a little shake from side to side (to mix the veggies with the water and sauce). Cover and cook for 4 hours, until very tender.

When you are ready to eat, place the brisket on a cutting board/sheet and remove any excess fat from the top (it will come off very easily-you can just scrape it off with a spoon and discard). Slice the brisket and place in your serving dish.

Place the cooked veggies around the brisket.

Add about 1 cup of very hot water to the pan. This helps create your sauce. Stir the sauce around, releasing any of those yummy bits from the bottom of the pan. Pour the sauce over your brisket and dig in!

Good Ole Chili

....

Serves 4-6.

I love a good bowl of chili. It may be reputed to be the quintessential cold weather food, but our family loves it almost anytime. This is the beef chili that I have been making for years. When I have experimented with other versions (what cook doesn't like to experiment?), my family wants to know why I tried to fix something that wasn't broken! Plan ahead since the chili cooks for at least 45 minutes.

3 lbs. lean ground beef (or a mix of ground beef and ground buffalo- a leaner choice)

1 medium onion, diced

15 oz. can tomato sauce

1 cup water

3 Tbsp. chili powder

1 Tbsp. dried oregano

1 Tbsp. ground cumin

½ tsp. garlic powder

1 tsp. cayenne pepper (less if you don't like it spicy)

1 tsp. paprika

½ tsp. salt

15 oz. can kidney beans (with few added ingredients), rinsed and drained

Place a large saucepan over medium heat and add the meat and onions. Cook until the meat is no longer pink, stirring occasionally. To drain the fat after the meat has browned, here's my technique:

Take the pan over to the sink. Put the top of the saucepan not quite on top of the pan, leaving a small opening at the top. Using a kitchen towel so you don't burn yourself, hold the top on with one hand on either side of the pot. Tilt the pan so you can pour off the fat without losing the meat.

Put the pot back over the heat. Add the remaining ingredients, except the beans, and stir. Bring to a boil and lower the heat to a simmer. Cover and simmer for 1 hour (30 minutes is o.k. if you are short on time). Add the beans and stir. Simmer for 15-20 more minutes. Tasty!

Louisiana Red Beans and Rice

....

Serves 4.

A Louisiana classic, this one pot meal is yummy, "stick-to-your-ribs" food with layers of flavor to perfectly complement the sausage and beans. And one of the best reasons to make this dish at home is that you get to control the quality of ingredients! I like to have some hot sauce handy to give it just that perfect kick.

1 lb. pure beef sausage-fully cooked (buy one with few ingredients, and lower fat, if possible), sliced into bite size pieces

1 Tbsp. canola oil

1 large onion, chopped

3 stalks celery, diced

4 good sized cloves garlic, minced

2 (15 oz.) cans red kidney beans, rinsed and drained

1 1/2 cups water

15 oz. can diced tomatoes with green chilies

1 Tbsp. Worcestershire sauce

¼ tsp. lemon pepper

¼ tsp. cayenne pepper (or, to taste)

1/2 tsp. Kosher salt

½ tsp. celery seed

1/2 tsp. garlic powder

½ tsp. oregano

2 bay leaves

1 cup rice (Uncle Ben's is best)

Heat a large saucepan/soup pot over medium-high heat.

Add the sausage and cook, stirring occasionally, until lightly browned (about 6 minutes). Remove the sausage, set aside, and pour any fat out of the pot (discard). Wipe the pot with a paper towel. Place the pot over medium heat to warm a bit, and add the canola oil, onions and celery. Stir. Cook until softened, about 6 minutes, stirring every once in a while.

Add the garlic and cook, while stirring, until fragrant, about 1 minute. Add the sausage, beans, water, tomatoes, and all of the remaining ingredients. Stir to combine. Bring to a boil.

Lower the heat to a simmer, and cook for 30 minutes.

Meanwhile, prepare rice (see Reliable Rice recipe).

Before you serve (or as you are serving), remove the bay leaves and discard.

Optional garnishes: hot sauce, chopped scallions

Tommy's Tacos

....

Serves 4-6.

Eating my husband's tacos is our Super Bowl Sunday tradition. They are DE-lish, and it's great to see him take over the kitchen as he checks on the taco shells, gently stirs his simmering concoction, dices the tomatoes, and mashes the avocados so that I can do my part- the guacamole! I like to make a taco salad for me, and black bean corn relish is the perfect topping (recipe follows)!

12-18 taco shells (some are healthier than others- go for the ones without a long list of ingredients)

3 lbs. extra lean ground beef

1/2 of a packet of taco spice mix from the store (e.g. Mc-Cormick)

Just under ½ cup of water

1 1/3 to 2 cups salsa (my husband uses 1/3 to ½ cup of 3 or 4 different salsas; use whatever combination/spiciness you like)

2 Tbsp. jalapenos, diced, (the pickled kind) or to taste, depending on how spicy you like to go

1 Tbsp. juice from jalapenos, if you want the kick

The juice from the diced tomatoes (see below)

Serve with:

3 medium tomatoes, diced pretty small (save the juice)

8 oz. cheddar cheese, grated

Lettuce of choice, washed, dried and chopped

1 recipe of Go-To Guacamole, optional

Preheat the oven to 250 degrees.

First, put the taco shells on a cookie sheet and place in the oven.

In a large skillet, over medium heat, brown the meat, stirring occasionally. To drain the fat, set the pan down near the sink and place the lid so it's covering the meat. Then, carefully tilt the pan so you can pour the fat off.

Put the skillet back over the heat. Add the taco spice, water, salsas, jalapeno, and jalapeno juice (if using) to the meat. Stir to combine. Dice the 3 medium tomatoes and add only the juices to the pan (set the tomatoes aside). Stir to combine. Bring to a boil, and then reduce to a simmer. Simmer until thickened, about 20-30 minutes. If you are in a hurry, you can cook at a more vigorous simmer and hurry the process along a bit, but slower is better.

Assemble the tacos and enjoy!

Note: This **Black Bean Corn Relish** goes really well with a taco salad or as a taco topper!

In a medium bowl, mix 2 (15 oz.) cans black beans (rinsed and drained), 1 ¼ cups frozen corn (cooked and drained)*, ½ a red bell pepper (diced), a little red onion or a small shallot (diced), a garlic clove (minced), some chopped cilantro to taste, 2-3 Tbsp. fresh lime juice, 1 Tbsp. olive oil, ½ tsp. sugar, ½ tsp. cumin, ½ tsp. dried oregano, and some pepper. Yum!

* If you would rather use fresh corn (2 ears), cut the corn off the cobb (see Silky Corn Chowder recipe for the technique).

Flank Steak with a Bite

....

Serves 4.

If you're in the mood for steak, this one is wallet friendly, easy to prepare, and cooks up very quickly. Just remember to plan ahead so the steak has time to marinate and absorb some of those garlic, lime juice, and spice flavors. Pair it with a simple salad, and some roasted corn or sweet potatoes and you're in for a really satisfying meal.

2 lb. flank steak, trimmed of extra fat

For the marinade:

2 Tbsp. canola oil

3 Tbsp. fresh lime juice

4 cloves garlic, minced

2 small fresh jalapenos, seeded (can see HELPING HAND) and diced (or less, if you like less heat)

½ tsp. cumin

1 tsp. paprika

1 tsp. chili powder

Whisk the marinade ingredients together in a small bowl.

Place the meat in a gallon size Ziploc bag and add the marinade. Seal the bag and massage it around a bit so all the meat is coated. Refrigerate for an hour or overnight, if time permits.

You can grill the meat or cook it in the oven. Avoid overcooking, because it makes flank steak become tough.

To grill: Remove the meat from the marinade and, on a clean, hot grill, cook the steak, turning once, until it's the doneness you like. About 15 minutes for medium. Let the steak rest on a platter for about 5 minutes to let the juices settle (can make a loose "tent" with foil and place over the meat to help keep it warm). Slice, thinly, across the grain and enjoy.

To cook in the oven: Remove meat from the marinade, and place in a broiler pan. Broil about 3" from heat for 5 to 8 minutes per side for medium doneness. Let the steak rest on a platter for about 5 minutes to let the juices settle (can make a loose "tent" with foil and place over the meat to help keep it warm). Slice, thinly, across the grain and enjoy.

Speedy Choc-Full-Of-Good Turkey Chili

....

Serves 2 generously.

For those who favor turkey chili, you can't beat this for speed and taste! My daughter and her friends have made it plenty of times and it's always a hit. Try it with some "It's a Keeper" Cornbread and a fresh green salad.

½ lb. ground turkey thighs (dark meat)

½ lb. ground turkey breast

14.5 oz. can diced tomatoes (with few added ingredients), with juices

½ can (the tomato can) water

1 Tbsp. plus 1 tsp. chili powder

1 tsp. garlic powder

¼ tsp. pepper

½ tsp. salt

¼ tsp. onion powder

½ tsp. ground cumin

1/8 tsp. cayenne pepper (more if you like more spice)

½ tsp. paprika

About 2/3 of a 15 oz. can kidney beans (with few added ingredients), rinsed and drained*

2/3 cup frozen corn, thawed most of the way

Cook the meat on medium heat in a medium saucepan until no longer pink, stirring occasionally.

To drain the fat after the meat has browned, here's my technique:

Take the pan over to the sink. Put the top of the saucepan not quite on top of the pan, leaving a small opening at the top. Using a kitchen towel so you don't burn yourself, hold the top on with one hand on either side of the pot. Tilt the pan so you can pour off the fat without losing the meat.

Put the pan back on medium heat. Add the tomatoes, ½ can of water, and the spices and stir. Bring to a boil. Lower the heat and simmer, covered, for 20 minutes. Add the beans and corn, and bring to a slow boil. Simmer for 10 minutes or until the beans and corn are thoroughly heated. Enjoy!

* The leftover beans: you could use them in a salad, or mash them with a fork and heat in a corn tortilla with a little cheese and salsa for a quick, healthy snack.

Parmesan Crusted Tilapia 3 Ways

....

Serves 4.

Tilapia is a mild fish that takes on other flavors very well. I created this simple recipe one day and then thought of two other easy ways to enjoy it- as fish tacos, and on a sandwich with homemade tartar sauce. I didn't know that this dish would assume its place as one of my husband's favorites! For easier cleanup, use paper plates for the parmesan and flour.

1 ½-2 lbs. tilapia (four 6-8 oz. pieces)

2 eggs plus 1 Tbsp. water, beaten

1 cup flour

1/4 tsp. pepper

1 cup grated parmesan cheese

2 Tbsp. Canola oil

Preheat the oven to 200 degrees.

Have a rimmed baking sheet and a large skillet ready to use. Beat the eggs and water in a medium bowl and set aside. Toss the flour and pepper together on a plate. Put the parmesan cheese in a separate plate. Now your station is ready.

Rinse the tilapia and pat dry with a paper towel.

Coat both sides of a piece fish with flour. Pat/shake it over the sink so the coating is very light. Dip the piece in the egg and let any excess drip off. Coat both sides with parmesan cheese.

Prepare 2 pieces (assuming your pan won't hold more without crowding), and heat 1 Tbsp. of oil in the skillet over medium heat for a minute or so ('til if you touch the edge of the fish to the oil, you hear a sizzle). Add the prepared tilapia.

Cook for about 5 minutes on one side, or until golden. Really get your spatula between the pan and the fish so the coating stays on and flip the fish. Cook for another 4 minutes or until golden and cooked through (can see HELPING HAND). Put the fish on your baking sheet and in the oven to keep warm, and repeat (adding another Tbsp. of oil to the pan) for the rest of the fish. Enjoy!

Have Fish Tacos:

Corn tortillas (buy ones with few ingredients)

1 large avocado, diced

For the Slaw:

2 cups cabbage (comes shredded and packaged at the store)

2 tsp. fresh lime juice

2 tsp. honey

2 Tbsp. minced scallions

1/8 tsp. cumin

2 tsp. minced, seeded jalapenos (or, to taste)

Pinch of salt

Put the slaw ingredients in a medium bowl and toss to combine.

Break the fish into chunks and serve up with corn tortillas, slaw, and avocado!

Have a Parmesan Crusted Tilapia sandwich with Homemade Tartar Sauce:

Good sourdough or bread of your choice, sliced

Fresh lettuce greens, optional

For the Tartar Sauce:

4 Tbsp. mayonnaise (I prefer Hellman's)

2 small dill pickles, minced

1/2 tsp. yellow mustard

1/4 tsp. onion powder

1 tsp. fresh lemon juice

1/8 tsp. Kosher salt

¼ tsp. pepper

A sprinkle of cayenne pepper (if you like a little kick)

Combine all of the ingredients in a small bowl and enjoy with your sandwich.

Crunchy Cod Sticks
with Homemade Horseradish Cocktail Sauce

....

Serves 4.

This recipe is inspired by the frozen fish sticks that we ate when I was little. Fish sticks with plenty of ketchup- I loved them! I recently had a craving for them, but wasn't very excited about making them from a box. So, this recipe, with a panko crunch and a horseradish spiked cocktail sauce was born.

1 ½ lbs. Cod (or Halibut, though it's usually pretty pricey)

½ cup flour

¼ tsp. salt

¼ tsp. pepper

3/4 cup panko bread crumbs

¾ cup grated parmesan cheese

3 egg whites, beaten (can see HELPING HAND for how to separate)

2 Tbsp. olive oil for drizzling

Cocktail sauce:

2/3 cup chili sauce (I like Heinz)

A good squirt of ketchup

1 Tbsp. prepared white horseradish

4-5 drops of Tabasco sauce

1 tsp. Worcestershire sauce

1 ½ tsp. fresh lemon juice

Preheat the oven to 400 degrees.
Spray a baking sheet well with Pam.

Set up your breading station:

Put the flour on a plate (use paper plates, if you like, for easier cleanup), add the salt and pepper, and mix with your fingers. Put the bread crumbs and parmesan on a different plate and mix with your fingers. Put the egg whites in a medium bowl and beat with a whisk or fork until a little frothy. You're set!

The procedure:

Rinse the fish, pat dry with a paper towel and cut into nice sized sticks (kind of the size of fried mozzarella sticks). Try to make them roughly the same size and thickness (so they will cook at about the same rate). Roll each fish stick in the flour and pat over the sink to get rid of the excess- you want it very lightly coated. Dip the floured fish in the egg whites and let the excess drip off. Roll in the breadcrumb/cheese mix, gently pressing the mixture into the fish, and place on your prepared baking sheet.

Drizzle the fish sticks with the olive oil. Bake until golden on the bottom, about 11 minutes. Flip with a metal spatula and cook until golden on top, about 11 minutes.

While the fish is cooking, make the cocktail sauce. Just place all the ingredients in a medium bowl and whisk to combine.

Enjoy!

David's Asian Style Salmon

....

Serves 4.

Our daughter's friend, David, is creative with food and loves to eat good food. So, he fits in well at the Samuels household. This salmon dish goes really well with Jasmine rice, baby bok choy, and sliced avocado. Try topping it with chopped scallions.

1 ½-2 lbs. salmon

Marinade:

¼ cup low sodium soy sauce

1/8 cup Mirin*

1 Tbsp. honey

1 Tbsp. olive oil

1 tsp. sesame oil

3 cloves garlic, minced

* Mirin is a Japanese cooking wine made from whole-grain sweet rice. It can be found in the Asian section at the store.

Preheat the oven to 400 degrees.
Have a 9x13 glass baking dish ready to go.

Whisk the marinade ingredients together in a small bowl. Reserve 3 Tbsp. and pour the rest of the mix into your baking dish. Rinse the salmon and pat dry with a paper towel. Place the salmon, skin side up, in the baking dish. Let it sit for 15 minutes (30 if you have time). Bake for 18 minutes, or until done (can see HELPING HAND). Flip the fish over with a metal spatula and brush with the remaining marinade mixture. Enjoy!

Grandma's Roasted Leg of Lamb

....

Serves 6-8.

I vividly remember the aroma that filled my husband's grandmother's house (everyone called her Grandma) on the days she was making her roasted leg of lamb. She served it along with her yellow squash casserole, potatoes au gratin, and very tasty mini croissants. It was always quite a meal, one that most often culminated with one of Grandma's homemade cream pies. Yum!

The lamb takes very little time to prepare. You just get it ready for the oven, and wait for the succulence to emerge. A meat thermometer is your "right hand man" on this one.

5-7 lb. leg of lamb, bone-in or boneless (boneless is easier to carve)

4 to 5 cloves of garlic, sliced thin

1/2 Tbsp. olive oil

Kosher Salt and pepper

Preheat the oven to 400 degrees.

Spray a roasting rack with Pam.

Have a roasting pan and a meat thermometer handy.

Cut through the packaging, being careful not to cut through the netting if you are using a boneless leg of lamb. Rinse the lamb and pat dry with paper towels. With a pointed tip knife, make slits all around the roast and insert the garlic slices as you go. Continue inserting the garlic until you have covered all surfaces of the meat.

Drizzle the oil on the lamb and rub gently all over. Sprinkle the lamb on all sides with a pretty good amount of salt and pepper (about 1 ½-2 tsp. each), and rub around with your fingers. Place the lamb on the roasting rack, fat side up. Cook on 400 for the first 20 minutes (this helps to seal the juices). Reduce the heat to 350. Then cook for 18-20 minutes per pound, until a meat thermometer reads 145 degrees, for medium rare to medium. If the roast is bone-in, be sure the thermometer doesn't touch the bone when you make your read.

Keep in mind that after you take the roast out, and while you let it rest for about 10 minutes (so the juices can redistribute), the temperature will rise about 5 degrees. If you cooked a boneless roast, cut the netting off. Slice the lamb roast with a sharp knife, and enjoy!

Always remember: If you're in the kitchen and you drop the lamb, you can always just pick it up. Who's going to know?

– Julia Child

This is every cook's opinion - no savory dish without an onion,
but lest your kissing should be spoiled, your onions must be fully boiled.

- Jonathan Swift

VEGGIES + *friends*

Confetti Israeli Couscous

....

Serves 6.

Israeli Couscous looks like little pearls, and has a nice "chew." Even people who are not couscous fans (my husband, for one) enjoy this different variety! The fruits and snap peas create a colorful look. The vinaigrette, with a touch of turmeric, and almond crunch totally round out the flavors.

One day, I planned to make this recipe, but my go-to stores didn't have any Israeli Couscous. So, I thought of an alternative: long grain brown rice.* It has the nutritious, high-fiber bran attached, and a nutty taste. While I'm partial to the couscous here, brown rice will work also.

1 Tbsp. olive oil

1 cup Israeli couscous

2 cups chicken or vegetable broth (mostly fat free is pretty easy to find)

1 cup chopped sugar snap peas, strings removed

1 granny smith apple, diced

¼ cup chopped sun dried tomatoes (the moist variety, not the ones packed in olive oil)

½ cup dried cranberries

1 medium mango, peeled and diced (can see HELPING HAND)

½ cup sliced almonds, toasted

Dressing:

3 Tbsp. red wine vinegar

3 Tbsp. olive oil

¼ tsp. Kosher salt

¼ tsp. pepper

¼ tsp. turmeric

Procedure:

Preheat the oven to 375 degrees.

Heat the olive oil in a medium saucepan over medium-medium high heat. Add the couscous and stir for 3-4 minutes, until the couscous is lightly browned. Slowly add the chicken or vegetable broth. Stir. Bring to a boil. Lower the heat to a simmer, cover, and cook for about 15 minutes, or until the liquid has been absorbed. Place the couscous in a large bowl (and spread out a bit with a spoon) to cool.

Make the dressing by whisking all the ingredients together in a small bowl. Set aside.

Spread the almonds out on a cookie sheet. Cook for about 7-8 minutes, until golden. If you start to smell them, they are ready! Cool on a plate.

To string the snap peas, pinch the very tip of the pea, getting hold of the string. Pull the string up the straightest side toward the stem end; pinch off the stem end and continue pulling until there is no more string. Chop and place in a medium bowl. Add the apples, sun dried tomatoes, cranberries, and mango to the bowl. Give the couscous a fluff with a fork. Add the fruit/veggie mixture, almonds, and dressing to the couscous. Stir gently to combine.

* If you can't find Israeli couscous, and decide to try this dish with long grain brown rice, just omit the 1 Tbsp. olive oil and cook the rice according to the package directions. Prepare the rest of the recipe as directed.

Whistler Mountain Roasted Carrots and Potatoes

....

Serves 6.

The inspiration for this dish came from the time my family took a gondola up to Whistler Mountain in Canada and was treated to a delicious chef-prepared dinner. That meal, coupled with chill-out time and amazing views - well, what do they say? "That's what memories are made of..."

5 medium potatoes (Yukon Golds work well)

6 medium carrots

10 garlic cloves, peeled (can see HELPING HAND)

½ tsp. dried thyme

½ tsp. dried oregano

½ tsp. Kosher salt

¼ tsp. pepper

1 tsp. balsamic vinegar (preferably a good one)

2 tsp. Worcestershire sauce

2 tsp. olive oil

2 tsp. Canola oil

1 ½ tsp. pure maple syrup (the real stuff)

Preheat the oven to 400 degrees.

Spray a 9x13 glass baking dish with Pam.

Wash the potatoes and carrots, and cut into medium size chunks (a little bigger than bite size). Put in a large bowl and add the remaining ingredients, except for the syrup. Toss together. Put in the baking dish and bake until the vegetables are tender and starting to turn a little golden, about 35 minutes. Stir the veggies once about half way through the cooking. Take the dish out of the oven and drizzle the maple syrup over the top. One more quick stir, and you're ready to go.

Classic Latkes (Potato Pancakes)

Serves 4-6.

Potato latkes are a traditional Chanukah favorite. True, many creative versions have popped up over the years, like sweet potato latkes, zucchini latkes, parsnip latkes, and apple potato latkes. Well, I am a traditionalist when it comes to latkes, so I present my classic recipe for your enjoyment. Our family likes it best with applesauce and sour cream on the side. Our kids often ask why I only make latkes at Chanukah time. No good reason! Actually, as a kid I would often watch my Mom make uber sized "potato pancakes" for my older brother to go with breakfast...

4 medium size potatoes (not baking potatoes-Yukon gold are good), grated

1 small onion, grated

4 Tbsp. flour

2 tsp. baking powder

2 eggs, beaten

1 1/4 tsp. salt

3 1/2 Tbsp. Canola oil for frying

Serve with: unsweetened applesauce and light sour cream on the side.

Preheat the oven to 200 degrees.

Have a cookie sheet, some paper towels for draining, and an ice cream scoop (kind with a release lever) handy. If you don't have such an ice cream scoop, you can form the potato pancakes with your hands.

Wash, dry (no need to peel), and grate the potatoes. If you have one, a food processor makes easy work of this. Put the potatoes in a large mixing bowl, giving handfuls a couple of squeezes as you go to get rid of excess liquid. Grate the onion over a plate. Give the grated onion a couple of squeezes with your hands to make them less juicy. Put the onion in the bowl with the potatoes. Add the remaining ingredients to the bowl and stir until well combined.

Heat a large skillet with 2 Tbsp. oil on just a tad higher than medium heat. When it has had about a minute to get hot, test with a bit of potato—see if when you touch it to the oil, it sizzles. If so, the oil is hot enough. Scoop the latkes mixture with your ice cream scoop. Press down on the top to pack the potatoes and release any extra juice*. Place in the skillet and gently push the top down with a spatula to flatten into a pancake (gently, or it might not hold together). You will probably be able to fry 4 good sized latkes at a time without overcrowding.

Fry until golden on one side (about 4 minutes), then flip and cook until golden on the other side. If you think the latkes are browning too fast, feel free to reduce the heat.

As the latkes come off the pan, set them down on a double layer of paper towels for a minute or so (to drain) and then place on a cookie sheet and put in the 200 degree oven to keep warm.

Before adding each new batch, remove any stray potato bits that have browned. Add about 1 to 1 1/2 Tbsp. oil to the pan and tilt the pan so the bottom is coated with oil. Repeat the process until all the latkes are ready.

* *Note*: liquid will accumulate at the bottom of your bowl - just avoid it as you scoop.

Sweet and Sour Okra

....

Serves 4.

My Mom is queen of Mediterranean specialties, including sweet and sour (her sweet and sour beef stew is amazing!). While many people, particularly in the South, think of fried as the main way okra is enjoyed, these tangy sweet flavors will not disappoint! Okra is also a good source of Vitamins A, B, and C.

1 lb. fresh okra, rinsed and chopped (can see HELPING HAND)

1 Tbsp. olive oil

2/3 cup diced onions

2 cloves garlic, minced

15 oz. can diced tomatoes (with few added ingredients)

1 ½ Tbsp. fresh lemon juice

1 Tbsp. brown sugar

2 Tbsp. ketchup

1/4 cup water

¼ tsp. salt

1/4 tsp. pepper

Prep your okra so it is ready to go. Heat a medium saucepan over medium heat. Add olive oil. Cook onion until it softens, about 3 minutes. Stir occasionally. Add the garlic and cook, while stirring, until fragrant, about one minute. Add the tomatoes, lemon juice, brown sugar, ketchup, water, salt, and pepper. Bring to a boil. Add the okra, bring to a boil again. Lower the heat to a simmer (gentle boil). Cover and cook until tender, about 15 minutes.

Broccolini with a Kick

....

Serves 4.

Broccolini, a cross between broccoli and Chinese broccoli, is definitely one of my favorites. It's similar to and vitamin rich like broccoli, yet sweeter in flavor, and more delicate in texture. Roasting it helps to bring out its natural sweetness.

2 bunches of broccolini

1 ½ Tbsp. olive oil

¼ tsp. Kosher salt

½ tsp. crushed red pepper (less if you don't like too much kick)

½ small lemon

2 Tbsp. grated parmesan cheese

Preheat the oven to 400 degrees.
Spray a rimmed baking sheet with Pam.

Wash the broccolini. Give it a few strong downward shakes over the sink to remove any excess moisture. Cut about 1/2 inch of the bottoms off.

Place the broccolini on the baking sheet. Drizzle the olive oil over the top. Sprinkle with salt and crushed red pepper flakes, and toss with your fingers to combine. Cook for about 6 minutes, or until tender (stalk can be easily pierced with a fork). Squeeze the juice from the lemon over the top and sprinkle with the parmesan cheese. Toss gently and serve.

Quick Sautéed Kale with Pumpkin Seeds and Garlic

Serves 2.

Don't worry if it seems like the recipe calls for a lot of kale. Like spinach, it wilts down to a fraction of its original volume. Kale has great antioxidant nutrients, and with this quick sauté, you'll enjoy great flavor and have the veggie part of your meal done in no time! I think this would go well mixed with a bowl of brown rice or quinoa, topped with chopped avocado, for a tasty vegetarian meal.

1 bunch kale (can see HELPING HAND for How to Select)

1 Tbsp. olive oil

2 cloves garlic, thinly sliced

1/2 cup vegetable stock or water

Pinch of salt

1/4 tsp. crushed red pepper flakes, optional

1 ½ tsp. red wine vinegar

2 Tbsp. roasted pumpkin seeds

Prep your kale as follows: Wash and just give the leaves (en masse) a few shakes over the sink. It's fine if some droplets cling to the leaves. Fold each leaf lengthwise, cut away the tough spines and discard. Tear the leaves or give them a rough chop (into pieces a little bigger than bite size). Put them in a bowl and set aside.

Heat the olive oil in a large saucepan over medium heat. Add the garlic and cook while stirring, until fragrant, about 1 minute (don't let it brown). Add the stock or water, salt, pepper flakes, if using, and kale and toss with tongs to combine. Cover and cook until just tender, about 4 minutes. Remove from the heat, add the vinegar, and toss to combine. Sprinkle with the pumpkin seeds and serve.

Simple Steamed Artichokes

....

Serves 2.

Slightly nutty tasting artichokes are a great addition to almost any meal. They may look a little mystifying, but they are really super easy to prepare. And they are loaded with fiber, low calorie, and have lots of antioxidants. If you don't know whether you're a fan, give them a try! Keep in mind that even though it's a super quick preparation, these do take about 30-45 minutes to cook, so plan ahead.

2 artichokes

Water

1 garlic clove, slightly smashed (lay your chef's knife on top of the clove and carefully give the flat side of the knife a whack)

2 slices of fresh lemon

1 bay leaf, optional

Optional: 2 Tbsp. melted butter for dipping the leaves and heart

Variation: dip the leaves in a mixture of olive oil and red wine vinegar (2 Tbsp. olive oil, 1 Tbsp. vinegar, salt and pepper to taste)

Pull off any smaller leaves toward the base and on the stems of the artichokes. Trim the stem to ½ inch in length. Rinse the artichokes under cold water.

Pour water into a large pot, to a depth of about 2 inches. Add the garlic, lemon, and bay leaf, if using. Insert a steaming basket if you have one (I've made these plenty of times without one). Put the artichokes in the pot, tips up. Bring the water to a boil. Reduce to a simmer, cover, and cook for 30 to 45 minutes or until the outer leaves can easily be pulled off and the base of the leaf is tender (see below for how to enjoy these and test one). You might want to check every once in a while to make sure the water level isn't getting too low. If so, just add a little more water.

Remove the artichokes from the pot and enjoy as follows: strip away an outer leaf and scrape away the meaty flesh at the base with your teeth. When you reach the center cone of prickly leaves (the choke that protects the heart), remove it. Now, scoop out and discard the inedible fuzzy center. What's left is the prized artichoke heart! Enjoy that!

Roasted Asparagus and
Cremini Mushrooms with Tomatoes and Feta

....

Serves 4.

The title may sound fancy, but this dish is super easy to prepare. The veggies, tomato, and feta combination is truly satisfying. Don't worry about the parsley garnish unless you want the dish to look totally gorgeous!

24 asparagus stalks

8 oz. Crimini (Baby Bella) mushrooms, sliced

1 Tbsp. olive oil

1/8 tsp. Kosher salt

¼ tsp. pepper

2/3 cup grape tomatoes or cherry tomatoes, halved

1/3 cup crumbled feta cheese

Garnish: 1 ½ Tbsp. fresh parsley, chopped

Preheat the oven to 400 degrees.

Spray a rimmed baking sheet with Pam.

Wash and dry the asparagus. Snap off the bottoms at the lowest spot that will snap off easily. As a short cut, you can just see where one snaps off most easily, and cut that much off of the rest of the asparagus bottoms. Cut into roughly 2 inch pieces and place in a medium size bowl. Wipe the mushrooms off with a damp paper towel (if you wash them with water, they will absorb too much moisture), cut off the very bottom of the stems, and discard. Slice the 'shrooms. Add those to the bowl with the asparagus. Add the olive oil, salt and pepper and toss gently with your fingers. Put the veggies on the baking sheet and cook for about 10-12 minutes. Basically, you want the asparagus to have a little bite to it (not get too limp) and still be bright green.

Meanwhile, prepare the tomatoes and feta and add to the bowl you mixed the asparagus and mushrooms in.

When the asparagus and mushrooms are done, remove the baking sheet from the oven and add the veggies to the tomatoes and cheese. Stir gently to mix. Transfer to a serving dish and sprinkle with parsley.

Farro and Roasted Butternut Squash with Cranberries and Walnuts

Serves 4.

Farro is an Italian whole grain packed with protein, fiber, and vitamins A, B, C, and E. It's been around for thousands of years, is delicious either warm or cold, and blends well with so many ingredients. It's technically in the wheat family, but people who have trouble with wheat tend to be able to tolerate farro. While I can usually find farro or quick cooking farro in grocery stores, sometimes I have trouble getting it. In that case, spelt or hulled barley would be a good alternative.

As for the butternut squash, it can be really tough to cut through unless your knives are good. Even then, it requires great care. I don't mean to scare you, you just need to careful. It's a cinch, of course, if you can buy butternut squash already peeled, chunked and ready to use! This dish is not only good looking. You'll definitely appreciate the chew and crunch of the farro and nuts, along with the creamy squash and cranberry touch of sweet.

This recipe uses half of a squash. Save the rest for a day later in the week (roast and eat as a side dish, or use in a salad).

For the butternut squash:

Half of one butternut squash (about 1 ½ lb.), peeled and cut into 3/4" cubes (see HELPING HAND)

1 ½ Tbsp. olive oil, divided

1 tsp. balsamic vinegar (preferably a good one)

Pinch Kosher salt

¼ tsp. pepper

For the farro:

1 cup farro, rinsed and drained

3 cups low sodium vegetable stock or water

1 tsp. salt (not Kosher)

Additional ingredients:

½ cup dried cranberries (dried cherries would be great also)

½ cup walnut pieces, toasted if you like*

2 Tbsp. parsley, chopped

¼ tsp. Kosher salt

Preheat the oven to 400 degrees.
Spray a rimmed baking sheet with Pam.

Place the butternut squash on the prepared baking sheet. Add 1/2 Tbsp. olive oil, balsamic vinegar, Kosher salt, and pepper. Toss with your fingers to combine. Spread in one layer and cook for about 16 minutes, or until golden and tender, stirring once.

Meanwhile, put the farro, stock or water, and salt in a medium saucepan. Stir and bring to a boil. Reduce to a simmer and cook until just tender, about 15 minutes. Drain and cool. *If you choose to toast the walnuts (they will be especially tasty!), heat a small skillet over medium heat. Add the nuts. Stir every so often. Once you start to smell them (about 4 minutes), they are ready.

In a large bowl, gently toss the farro, butternut squash, cranberries, walnuts, parsley, Kosher salt, and 1 Tbsp. olive oil.

Sautéed Bok Choy with Sunflower Seeds

Serves 4.

I love bok choy. It's crunchy, light, and totally versatile! It's also really low in calories, and is a good source of Calcium, Vitamin A, and Vitamin C. This dish goes very well with David's Asian Style Salmon and a side of Jasmine Rice.

Have a large skillet ready to go.

3 bunches of baby bok choy (I prefer these), or 1 head of mature (large) bok choy (can see HELPING HAND for Selecting and Preparing)

1 tsp. sesame oil

½ Tbsp. olive oil

1/8 tsp. Kosher salt

1/8 tsp. pepper

1 ½ Tbsp. sunflower seeds

Cut off the root end of the bok choy and separate the leaves while holding the bok choy under running water until all visible dirt has been washed away (for baby bok choy, you can leave the tender baby that's in the middle intact). Give the leaves a little shake over the sink to get rid of excess water.

Cut the celery-like stalks into 1 inch pieces. For mature bok choy, slice the leaves into ribbons.

Heat a skillet over medium-high heat. Add the oils once the pan is hot. Add the bok choy and the salt and pepper. Cook for about 3 minutes, tossing with tongs, until the leaves are just wilted and the stalks are crisp-tender. The stalks of mature bok choy take longer to cook, so for those, add the stalk pieces first, cook for about 3 minutes, then add the leaves and cook for another 2 minutes (all while tossing occasionally with tongs). Transfer to your serving plate, and sprinkle the sunflower seeds over the top. Delish!

No-Cook-Noodle Kugel (Noodle Pudding)

Serves 8.

Kugel is a quintessentially Jewish comfort food best described as baked pudding. As recipes have been passed on for generations, there is a wide variety of preparations (e.g. sweet or savory, dense to fluffy, some creative topping choices). My favorite is made with this classic blend of velvety noodles, sour cream, butter, and a touch of warm spice. Decadent? Often, quite. But this recipe has been lightly tweaked. It is also quicker to prepare because the noodles don't need to be precooked. Try serving it warm with brunch or as a side dish anytime.

8 oz. wide egg noodles (don't use more)

1/3 cup chopped dried apricots*

5 eggs

1 ¼ cups light sour cream

½ cup sugar

4 Tbsp. butter, melted

1 tsp. vanilla

1 tsp. cinnamon

½ tsp. nutmeg

½ tsp. salt

4 cups low fat milk (1%, even skim, is fine)

Topping:

1/3 cup sliced almonds

1 Tbsp. of brown sugar

Preheat the oven to 350 degrees.

Spray a 9x13 glass baking dish with Pam.

Spread the noodles in the baking dish. Distribute the apricots over the top. Whisk the eggs, sour cream, sugar, butter, vanilla, cinnamon, nutmeg, and salt until well combined. Whisk in milk and pour the mixture over the noodles. With your fingers or a spoon, submerge any big noodle corners sticking out of the mixture so they won't get over crispy when cooking. Let stand for 6 minutes. Sprinkle the almonds and brown sugar over the noodles. Bake about 45-50 minutes or until just set (not jiggly) in the middle. Serve warm or at room temp.

Variation: Feel free to substitute other dried fruits, such as raisins, dried cherries, blueberries, or cranberries. You could also add 1 tsp. ground cardamom instead of the nutmeg.

Dijon-Roasted Cauliflower with Red Pepper and Walnuts

Serves 4.

I happen to love cauliflower. I think it's probably most tasty when fried (let's be honest!), but roasting it makes it taste almost the same. So, even though cauliflower roasted to a deep golden hue with a bit of olive oil, salt, and pepper is pretty delicious all by itself, I wanted a little flavor twist. The Dijon, red pepper, and walnut crunch play the part nicely!

1 head of cauliflower, cut into pretty even sized florets (can see HELPING HAND for Selecting and Preparing)

1 small red bell pepper, chopped

1/3 cup walnuts, chopped and toasted

For the marinade:

2 Tbsp. Olive oil

2 tsp. Dijon mustard

1 tsp. fresh lemon juice

¼ tsp. Kosher salt

¼ tsp. pepper

1/8 tsp. cayenne pepper (if you like a little kick)

Preheat the oven to 400 degrees.
Spray a rimmed baking sheet with Pam.

Toast the walnuts: put the nuts on a cookie sheet and cook for 7-10 minutes (if you start to smell them, they are ready). Shake the pan halfway through. Remove from the oven, place the nuts on a plate and set aside.

Place the marinade ingredients in a large bowl and whisk to combine. Add the cauliflower and red pepper and toss together with your fingers. Transfer to the baking sheet, and cook for about 20-25 minutes, stirring about halfway through. You want the cauliflower to be golden brown. Transfer to your serving dish, top with toasted walnuts, and serve.

Acorn Squash with Brown Sugar and Butter

Serves 4.

It seems people always love this dish, maybe since it tastes almost like dessert. It is good looking and is very easy to prepare. On top of that, it's a great source of Vitamins A and C.

1 medium acorn squash, about 2 lbs. (can see HELPING HAND for Selecting and Preparing)

1 Tbsp. butter

½ Tbsp. brown sugar

Sprinkle of cinnamon

Slice the squash in half, stem to end, with a good chef's knife. To make the squash easier to cut, pierce the skin in a few spots (carefully, with the end of a paring knife) and place it on a microwave safe plate, and in the microwave for 2 minutes. Let it stand for another few minutes before cutting.

Scoop the seeds and stringy pulp out of the squash cavities and discard. Place the squash halves on a microwave safe plate and cook, flesh side down, until tender, about 15 minutes. You want them to feel kind of the same as a baked potato that is ready to eat. I place a kitchen towel over the squash (to protect my hand from the heat) and give it a squeeze.

OR, if you want a caramelized glaze around the squash, preheat the oven to 400 degrees. Spray a rimmed baking sheet well with Pam. Drizzle 1 tsp. olive oil over each squash half (and rub around). Roast flesh side down for 30 minutes, or until tender.

When the squash halves are cool enough to handle, turn them over, and slice each in half (into crescent shapes). Place on a serving plate, rub the butter over all surfaces of each piece, leaving a dab in the middle of each. Distribute the brown sugar on top of the 4 pieces, and sprinkle with a touch of cinnamon. Enjoy!

Swiss Chard with Apricots, Green Olives, and Goat Cheese

Serves 4.

Swiss Chard is extraordinarily nutrient-rich, and palette pleasing too! The stalks come in red, white, and yellow, with white being the most tender (I love the red, partly because it is so pretty). The creamy goat cheese, salty olives, and sweet apricots are a great foil for the chard in this dish.

2 bunches Swiss chard (about 1 lb.), stalks and leaves separated, and chopped into roughly bite-sized pieces (can see HELPING HAND for Selecting and Preparing)

1 Tbsp. olive oil

1/8 teaspoon salt

1/4 teaspoon freshly ground pepper

1/4 cup chopped pitted green olives

1/4 cup chopped dried apricots

1/3 cup crumbled goat cheese

Wash and prep your chard leaves and stalks. It's fine for some of the water to cling to the leaves as it helps steam the chard.

Heat olive oil in a large saucepan over medium heat. Add chard stalk pieces (they take longer to cook than the leaves do), salt, and pepper and cook, stirring often, until softened, 3 to 5 minutes. Stir in chard leaves and cook, stirring constantly, until wilted, about 2 minutes. Stir in olives and apricots. Dot goat cheese over the top, cover and cook until the chard is tender and the cheese is melted, about 1-2 minutes more.

Roasted Root Vegetable Melange

....

Serves 4-6.

Roasting root vegetables brings out their natural sweetness and intensifies their natural flavors. These veggies are nutritional storehouses, with great vitamins, minerals, and fiber. If you are unfamiliar with selecting and preparing some of these veggies, consult the Helping Hand section. A good chef's knife makes easy work of the chopping!

Plan ahead a bit since these cook for about 45 minutes.

½ lb. celeriac (celery root)

½ lb. carrots

½ lb. parsnips

½ lb. turnips

½ lb. rutabaga

2 Tbsp. olive oil

1 Tbsp. butter, melted

1 ½ Tbsp. whole grain mustard

½ tsp. Kosher salt

¼ tsp. pepper

Preheat the oven to 350 degrees.

Spray a rimmed baking sheet with Pam.

Peel* and chop the veggies into ¾" cubes. Place them in a large bowl. Add the olive oil, butter, mustard, salt, and pepper and stir to combine. Transfer to your baking sheet and cook for about 45 minutes, stirring mid-way, until tender and golden.

*You don't have to peel the carrots or young parsnips- it's up to you. And, if the turnips are young and small (golf ball sized), they don't need to be peeled. Just give those veggies a good scrubbing.

Spaghetti Squash with Almonds, Parsley, and Garlic

....

Serves 4.

People eating low carb or those who just want an alternative to traditional pasta must discover this star vegetable! It's fun to make, delicious, and I love how versatile it is. I have made it with tomatoes and mozzarella (topped with turkey Bolognese), with shiitake mushrooms, sweet potatoes, and garlic, and tossed with lots of fresh veggies, a la pasta primavera.

Plan ahead since the squash cooks for about 30 minutes.

2 whole spaghetti squashes, about 1 pound each (or one, about 2 lb.)

2 tsp. olive oil

¼ cup sliced almonds

½ Tbsp. butter

3 cloves garlic, minced

1/4 cup chopped parsley

1 small scallion (white and green part), minced

1/4 tsp. Kosher salt

¼ tsp. crushed red pepper flakes (or to taste)

1 Tbsp. fresh lime juice

Preheat the oven to 400 degrees.

Slice the squash in half lengthwise and remove the seeds with a spoon. Place on a rimmed baking sheet drizzle with olive oil, and turn cut-side down. Roast until tender (can easily pierce with a fork), about 30 minutes. Meanwhile, spread the almonds on a second baking sheet and toast in the oven, until golden, about 3 minutes.

Heat a small skillet over medium-low heat. Add butter and garlic. Cook until sizzling some and garlic is soft (don't let it turn brown), about 5 minutes. Chop the parsley and scallion. Since the squash will be hot, hold it with a dish towel and use a fork to scrape out the pasta-like strands. Transfer the strands to a colander and press down a bit so any extra water will be released. Put the strands into a medium bowl. Add the garlic, parsley, scallions, salt, crushed red pepper, and lime juice. Toss with tongs until well mixed. Sprinkle with almonds and you're good to go.

Brussels-y Love

....

Serves 4.

Many people have a tendency to wrinkle their nose (or entire face!) at the mention of Brussels sprouts. Actually, they are pretty "in" right now, perhaps owing to master chefs fancying up their prep. That said, like I often tell my son (particularly about squash, which he seems determined not to like in any form), "Just try it. It may surprise you." If you are already a fan, I think you'll love this preparation - roasted with a touch of balsamic, parmesan cheese, and lemon!

1 lb. Brussels sprouts (look for unblemished bright green sprouts with compact leaves - can see HELPING HAND)

1 ½ Tbsp. olive oil

1 tsp. balsamic vinegar (preferably a good one)

Pinch Kosher salt

¼ tsp. pepper

1 Tbsp. grated parmesan cheese

Juice from ½ small lemon

Preheat the oven to 375 degrees.

Spray a rimmed baking sheet with Pam.

Remove any raggedy outer leaves from the Brussels sprouts and slice off any large stem ends. Wash them well. Cut in half from stem to top. Place on the baking sheet and add the olive oil, balsamic vinegar, salt, and pepper. Toss with your fingers so that all the sprouts are well coated. Cook until the sprouts are fork tender and some of the leaves have become golden, about 20 minutes. Toss once during cooking.

Transfer the sprouts to your serving bowl. Sprinkle with parmesan cheese, squeeze the lemon over the top, toss, and enjoy.

Hoppin' Johns (Black Eyed Peas)

....

Serves 8.

Eating Hoppin' Johns (black eyed peas) on New Year's Day is an old Southern tradition. Grandma, quite the Southern lady, always had the family over for Hoppin' Johns and other delicious treats. My husband, Tom, wanted to continue the tradition, and we happily have done so!

One of the tales about how Hoppin' Johns got its name says that a man named John came "a-hoppin'" when his wife took the dish from the stove. Surely, he wanted some of the good luck that they represent as the New Year began!

After the Hoppin' Johns are ready, I normally add some turkey sausage (one with few added ingredients) that I have browned in a skillet. Grandma always served the black eyed peas over rice, and since I know Uncle Vic will be looking for some Tobasco sauce, I am sure to have that on hand as well.

Add a pan of warm "It's a Keeper" Cornbread (either plain, or jalapeno cheddar) to your spread and you'll have some happy people chowing down!

2 (11 oz.) containers fresh black eyed peas (or 2 cups dried*)

4 cups water

1 small onion, diced

2 stalks celery, diced

½ tsp. garlic powder

¼ tsp. cumin

2 bay leaves

1/2 tsp. Kosher salt

½ tsp. pepper

Optional: Brown 3/4 lb. of turkey or chicken sausage (I use a good quality "fully cooked" variety), sliced, in a skillet and add to the black eyed peas after they are cooked.

Optional: Serve over brown rice (Success brand pouches are easy!) or white rice (see recipe for Reliable Rice)

Garnish with: Tabasco or Louisiana Hot Sauce, chopped green onions, and/or chopped tomatoes.

Rinse and drain the black eyed peas. Put them in a large soup pot. Add the water, onions, celery, garlic powder, cumin, bay leaves, salt, and pepper.

Stir. Remove any peas that float. Bring to a boil. Lower the heat to a simmer and cook for about 15-18 minutes, until the peas are tender, but not mushy.

As the peas cook, skim off any grayish foam (impurities from the beans) off the top with a large spoon and discard. It's easiest if you guide it over to one side of the pot and remove. If you are using sausage, heat 1 Tbsp. olive oil in a large skillet and add the sausage. Cook just 'til browned on both sides (the sausage is already cooked). Set aside.

When the peas are done, remove and discard the bay leaves, and add the sausage, if using. Stir and enjoy!

Note: If you use dried, sort through the peas and remove any small stones or debris. You can use the "quick soak" method to cut down on cooking time. Just put the peas in 2 cups of boiling water, boil for 2 minutes, and soak for 1 hour. Discard the soaking liquid and proceed with the recipe. These take a little longer to become tender, about 30-40 minutes.

Stir Fried Snow Peas with Shiitakes and Sesame Seeds

....

Serves 4.

Snow peas are crunchy, light, versatile, and cook up in no time. And, shiitakes are one of my favorite mushrooms. While they are sometimes kind of pricey, I think the incredible earthy flavor and slightly chewy texture make them worth it! The combo works really nicely with the Asian-inspired flavors in this recipe.

12-16 medium shiitake mushrooms

3 cups snow peas

2 garlic cloves, minced

1 Tbsp. Canola oil

½ tsp. sesame oil

1 tsp. soy sauce, preferably low sodium

¼ tsp. pepper

Pinch of Kosher salt

1 tsp. toasted sesame seeds (in the spice section at the store)

Wipe the mushrooms with a damp paper towel. Cut off the very bottom of the stems (discard), and slice the 'shrooms. Break off the stem end of each pea and pull the string away from the pod. Cut the snow peas in half if they are large. Prep your garlic. Heat a medium skillet over medium-high heat. Add the Canola oil. Swirl to coat the pan. When the oil is hot, add the mushrooms in a single layer, and cook for about 4 minutes, until they begin to turn golden. Stir. Add the snow peas, sesame oil, soy sauce, garlic, pepper, and pinch of salt. Cook for 4 minutes more, while stirring. Transfer to a serving plate, sprinkle with the sesame seeds, and enjoy!

Reliable Rice

....

Serves 4.

For dishes that go well served over rice, such as Good Ole Chili or Hoppin' Johns, this is your basic recipe.

2 cups water

1 cup long grain rice (Uncle Ben's is best)

1/4 tsp. salt

Add the water, rice and salt to a medium saucepan over medium-high heat. Stir to combine. Bring to a boil. Lower the heat to a simmer (gentle boil), cover, and cook until the water is absorbed, about 20 minutes.

One Variation: Use chicken stock instead of water for added flavor.

Another Tasty Variation: Stir 1/3 cup dried cranberries or raisins and 1/3 cup toasted slivered almonds (can see HELPING HAND for how to toast) into the rice just before serving.

Red Rice

....

Serves 4.

Red rice was my Dad's specialty. When he made it at our house to go with dinner, I would get the ingredients and the right pot and wooden spoon out for him. Then he would work his magic! While I have modified the recipe to make it simpler (no soaking the rice and less cooking time), it is still delicious and so wonderful with many meals.

A Middle Eastern favorite way to prepare the rice is to have a layer on the bottom that forms a crispy, almost burned, crust. When I cook it that way, Dad's and my favorite, I always think of how much he would have loved it!

1 1/2 cups water

8 oz. can tomato sauce (with few added ingredients)

1 ½ Tbsp. Canola oil

1 cup long grain rice (Uncle Ben's is best)

¼ tsp. salt

Put the water, tomato sauce, oil, rice, and salt in a medium saucepan over medium-high heat. Stir to combine. Bring to a boil. Lower the heat to a simmer (gentle boil), cover, and cook until the liquid is absorbed, about 25 minutes.

Mexican Rice

....

Serves 4.

This rice dish is perfect either with a Mexican themed dinner or just as a side dish when you want rice with a little extra flavor. The veggies add color and texture; the spices and tomato make the dish complete!

2 cups water

8 oz. can tomato sauce

1 Tbsp. Canola oil

1 cup long grain rice (Uncle Ben's is best)

¼ tsp. salt

¼ tsp. cumin

¼ tsp. chili powder

¼ tsp. garlic powder

1 cup frozen mixed vegetables, thawed most of the way in the microwave

Add all of the ingredients, except the mixed vegetables, to a medium saucepan over medium-high heat. Stir to combine. Bring to a boil. Lower the heat to a simmer (gentle boil), cover, and cook for 15 minutes. Add the mixed vegetables and stir to combine. Bring to a simmer, cover and cook until the rest of the liquid is absorbed, about 10-12 minutes.

Jasmine Rice

....

Serves 4.

Jasmine rice really does taste different than normal long grain white rice. It's a treat if you pay attention to savoring the delicate flavor. Try this with David's Asian Style Salmon, Sautéed Bok Choy, and avocado slices on the side.

1 cup jasmine rice

1 ¾ cups water

¼ tsp. salt

Place the rice in a large bowl and rinse with 2 or 3 changes of cold water. To drain the rice, either do your best to cover the rice with your hand while tilting the bowl (so you don't lose too much rice), or use a sieve/colander. Bring the water and salt to a boil, add the rice, and stir. Bring to a boil again, and reduce heat to a simmer. Cover and cook for about 20 minutes, or until the water has been absorbed. Remove from heat and set aside, covered, for 10 minutes. Fluff rice with a fork before serving.

"It's a Keeper" Corn Bread (Plain or Jalapeno Cheddar)

Serves 8.

This is a favorite in our house when we have Good Ole Chili and when we celebrate New Year's Day with Hoppin' Johns (black eyed peas). My better-for-you version with a secret touch of butternut squash comes out just as moist and delicious as richer varieties! It's always a hit.

1 cup flour

1 cup stone ground corn meal

1 tsp. salt

4 tsp. baking powder

¼ cup brown sugar (packed)

3 Tbsp. jarred baby food butternut squash (2.5 oz.)

1 Tbsp. canola oil

2 eggs

1 cup 1% milk

For Jalapeno Cheddar Corn Bread, add:

¼ cup sliced jalapenos

½ cup lower fat (2%) cheddar cheese

Of course, just add one if that's what you prefer.*

Preheat the oven to 350.

Spray a 8x8 baking pan with Pam.

Put the flour, corn meal, salt, baking powder, and sugar in a medium bowl. Stir to combine (smushing any clumps of brown sugar with the back of your spoon). Set aside. Put the squash, oil, eggs, and milk in a larger bowl and whisk to combine. Add the dry to the wet ingredients and stir until combined. If you are using the jalapenos and/or cheddar cheese, add that/those ingredients and stir again, just until combined. Transfer to your baking pan. Bake for 24 minutes or until a toothpick inserted in the center comes out without batter attached.

Note: Sometimes my family wants half plain and half jalapeno cheddar. What I do is pour the batter in the pan, as usual. Over half of the batter, I scatter 1/3 cup cheese and 1/8 cup (or, to taste) of jalapenos. Then, with a smallish spoon, I gently stir the cheese and jalapenos into that half, trying not to scrape bottom. It works!

Balsamic Roasted Sweet Potatoes

....

Serves 4.

Sweet potatoes aren't just for Thanksgiving! And, remember, the more colorful the veggies, the better they are for you. You can have these in the oven in not much longer than it takes you to chop the potatoes. Enjoy them just like this (as a side dish), or be creative! I have enjoyed roasted sweet potatoes in a salad, mixed with spaghetti squash, parsley and garlic as a main dish, and with shiitake mushrooms in a scramble.

4 small or 2 medium sweet potatoes, scrubbed and chopped into ½ inch cubes

1 Tbsp. olive oil

1 Tbsp. balsamic vinegar (preferably a good one)

¼ tsp. Kosher salt

¼ tsp. pepper

Preheat the oven to 400 degrees.

Spray a rimmed baking sheet with Pam.

Put the potatoes, olive oil, balsamic vinegar, salt, and pepper in your prepared baking sheet. Toss with your fingers. Spread into a single layer and cook for about 20 minutes, stirring once, until the potatoes are tender and the crispness that you like.

Variation: To make some incredible plain **roasted potatoes**, cut 8 small red potatoes into ½ inch cubes. Proceed as above, omitting the balsamic and increasing the salt to ½ tsp.

What I say is that if a man really likes potatoes, he must be a pretty decent sort of fellow.

- A.A. Milne

Let's face it, a nice creamy chocolate cake does a lot for a lot of people. It does for me.

\- Audrey Hepburn

sweeeeet RECIPES

Shortbread Jam Cookies

Makes about 32 small cookies.

The thumbprint cookies my Mom made while I was growing up were my absolute favorite! While she doesn't bake much these days, I am happy to take over with this very close (and healthier) recipe. Feel free to substitute your favorite jam. The buttery goodness takes me back…

You'll need some parchment paper (mostly for easier clean-up in case the jam runs).

1 cup almond meal/flour

1 ½ cups whole-wheat pastry flour

½ cup brown sugar

1 ½ tsp. baking powder

10 Tbsp. butter, room temperature*

1 egg

About 3½ Tbsp. good raspberry preserves (one with few ingredients, like just raspberries, sugar and pectin)

Optional garnish: a light dusting of powdered sugar

Preheat the oven to 400 degrees.

Line 2 baking sheets with parchment paper.

Put the flours, sugar, and baking powder in a large bowl and whisk to combine. Add the butter and mix in with your fingertips until crumbly (resembles small peas). Lightly beat the egg in a small bowl, and add to the flour/butter mixture. Stir with a wooden spoon to blend into a dough.

If you divide the dough in half, then in half again, and make about 8 cookies from each piece (they will be about 1 Tbsp. size), the recipe will make about 32 small cookies. Roll the dough into balls and place on the cookie sheet. Make an indentation in the middle and fill with jam (use a small spoon).

Try to make a tiny rim all around the indentation so the jam won't dribble out as the cookies bake. I have heard that some people use the top of a chapstick tube as a trick for creating the indentation… One of my recipe testers used the back of a ¼ tsp. measure.

Bake the cookies until lightly golden around the edges, about 11-12 minutes. Cool on a rack.

*Who has butter at room temp?

My trick is to use the microwave. I leave the butter in its wax paper wrapping, and heat in small second increments, starting with 12 seconds (then 4), until soft. Do it slowly so the butter doesn't melt!

Peace Cookies

....

Makes about 40 cookies.

I call these Peace Cookies because they are pretty "granola". They have an awesome flavor layered with oats, cranberries, coconut, and nuts, and a very satisfying crunch! They also freeze well. My daughter and her boyfriend like to take these with them whenever they go hiking or camping. So, whether you're in need of a wholesome pick-me-up, or you just want to eat a great cookie, these are it!

One hint: Store the flax seeds in the freezer. They will last longer there.

1 ¼ cups whole wheat pastry flour

½ tsp. baking soda

½ tsp. salt

1 tsp. cinnamon

½ cup butter, softened*

1 cup brown sugar, packed

1 egg

½ tsp. lemon zest (just the yellow part of the skin, no white)

2 cups oats (not quick cooking type)

¼ cup dried cranberries (or dried cherries)

¼ cup flax seeds

¼ cup, sweetened shredded coconut

½ cup nuts (I used a mixture of unsalted cashews, slivered almonds, and walnuts), chopped (can see HELPING HAND for how to chop)

Preheat the oven to 350 degrees. Have a cookie sheets(s) ready to use.

Stir the flour, baking soda, salt, and cinnamon together in a medium bowl and set aside.

With your electric mixer (or, by hand, with a wooden spoon), beat the butter and sugar together until creamy (about 2 minutes). Add the egg and lemon zest and mix until combined. Add the flour mixture to the butter mixture and stir with a wooden spoon until combined. Stir in the oats, cranberries, flax seeds, coconut, and nuts.

Place a ball of dough on your ungreased cookie sheet- a little smaller than golf ball size- and flatten slightly (I just use my fingers) . I fit 20 cookies on a sheet.

Bake for about 16-18 minutes, until golden around the edges. You can let them get golden on top if you like your cookies really crunchy.

While the cookies are baking, if you have another cookie sheet, get that one ready to go in the oven when the first cookies come out. Let the cookies cool for a bit on the cookie sheet and then on a wire rack. Yum!

*Who wants to wait for the butter to come to room temp?!

My trick is to use the microwave. I leave it in its wax paper wrapping, and heat in small second increments, starting with 12 seconds (then 4), until soft. Do it slowly so the butter doesn't melt.

Mmmmmm Brownies

....

Makes 9 large brownies.

These brownies are fudgy and delicious. They contain about half the butter that most brownies do, but you won't find them lacking in taste or texture. And, they are so easy to prepare...

¼ cup flour

½ tsp. baking powder

¼ tsp. salt

8 oz. semi-sweet chocolate chips, plus ¼ cup for sprinkling

4 Tbsp. butter

2 Tbsp. from jar of sweet potatoes baby food (you can add leftover to a smoothie)

2 eggs, beaten

1/3 cup sugar

1 tsp. vanilla

Preheat the oven to 350 degrees.

Spray a 9x9 pan with Pam (Note that the recipe was tested using a 9x9 pan, but if you only have an 8x8, just increase the cooking time by about 3-4 minutes and check frequently for doneness).

Combine the flour, baking powder and salt in a small bowl and set aside. In a large microwave safe bowl melt 8 oz. of chocolate and the butter in the microwave (start with 45 seconds, check, and continue with small increments of time, just until melted). Stir together until smooth. Add the sweet potatoes (give the baby food jar a little stir first) and stir with a whisk to combine. Add the eggs, sugar, and vanilla and stir with a whisk until the eggs are incorporated.

Add the flour mixture to the chocolate mixture and fold* together with a rubber spatula, just until the flour mixture is fully incorporated.

*Folding is a kind of stirring.

It's just a little different (and more delicate) in that rather than the usual way of stirring, you want to kind of hold the spatula at a 45 degree angle to the bowl and fold the mixture over itself in a rolling kind of motion until the flour mixture is incorporated.

Transfer to your baking pan. Scatter the ¼ cup of chocolate chips over the top. Cook for 12-14 minutes. The top will look barely cooked and the edges will look done. A toothpick inserted in the middle shouldn't come out all goopy, but won't be completely clean either. Don't over-bake!

In a Jiff Flourless Peanut Butter Cookies

....

Makes 32 small cookies.

Crunchy, peanut-y goodness. That's how I describe these flourless cookies that you can whip up in no time. While flax seeds are not actually a grain, they offer a great nutrient payload similar to the vitamin and mineral profile of grains. If you store the ground flax seed in an airtight container in the freezer, it will keep better. Also, in terms of other uses for ground flax seed, try adding some to homemade muffins, breads, protein shakes, smoothies, or sprinkle some on cooked vegetables or hot cereal (do this at the end of cooking since the soluble fiber in the flaxseeds can thicken liquids if left too long).

See the option below for making half the batch into peanut butter chocolate chip cookies. Yumm!

3/4 cup peanut butter (I tested with Laura Scutter's "All Natural" Crunchy - just peanuts and salt)*

2 Tbsp. ground flax seed

3/4 cup sugar

¼ cup oats (not the quick cooking kind)

1 egg

Preheat the oven to 350 degrees.

Spray a cookie sheet well with Pam (or, better yet, line your cookie sheet with parchment paper).

Stir/kind of mash all of the ingredients together with a wooden spoon until well mixed. Drop by spoonfuls onto your cookie sheet (I used a spoon like you would stir coffee with). You'll have enough for 2 pans of 16 cookies.

Make the classic peanut butter cookie "design" on each cookie as follows: press the tines of a fork onto the cookie in one direction, then in the other direction, creating a criss-cross pattern. When the fork starts sticking to the cookies, pour some water into a shallow plate, dip the fork in the water, give it a little shake, and continue. Bake for 15 minutes, or until golden on the bottom, and slightly golden on top. Tasty!

Variation: Peanut Butter Chocolate Chip Cookies

Add 1/3 cup chocolate chips to half of the dough and mix together. Form them with your hands into small balls, and place on the cookie sheet. Gently flatten the cookies only slightly. Bake as above.

Here's my trick to make stirring the peanut butter easier:

I just turn the jar upside down and leave it on the kitchen counter. A couple of hours later, or, after a while (whenever I pass by), I turn it upside down again (and repeat). This really helps pre-mix it a little. Of course, if you are going to use it right away, the stirring just takes longer…

Choc-O-Squares

....

Makes about 18 servings.

A family favorite, choc-o-squares are a one bowl wonder. The "secret" is all in the baking. If you don't overcook them, they are a melt-y chocolate-coconut-walnuts party in your mouth! They freeze well, so tasty treats can be on hand when the craving strikes.

1 ½ cups graham cracker crumbs (the less ingredients the better)

1 cup sweetened (shredded for baking) coconut

12 oz. semi-sweet chocolate chips

1 cup walnut pieces

1 14 oz. can sweetened condensed milk (I use Eagle brand)

1 stick butter, melted

Preheat the oven to 325 degrees.

Spray a 11x7 glass baking dish with Pam.

Mix all the ingredients together in a large bowl. Transfer to the pan and spread with the back of a metal spoon so that the top is even. Bake for 30-33 minutes. It should look slightly golden around the edges, but it will not feel firm to the touch (you want it to end up a little gooey inside). Also, when you take it out of the oven, as it sits, it will firm up a bit. Slice into squares and enjoy!

Fudge-y Flourless Chocolate Cake

....

Serves 10.

Flourless chocolate cake is almost a necessity for your baking repertoire! This recipe is easy, richly chocolate-y and even boasts a calcium and protein boost from the almonds. It's one of those tastes-like-you-worked-hard recipes. While almond meal can be kind of pricey, it comes in handy- try the Amazing Flourless Banana Bread or Shortbread Jam Cookie recipes. Or, add some to your smoothies. Fresh berries are the perfect accompaniment for this dessert.

You'll need some parchment paper.

To prepare the cake pan:

Butter the bottom and sides of a 9 inch cake pan (use a paper towel to hold the butter if you don't want to get messy). Lay a sheet of parchment paper (a little bigger than the cake pan) on the counter. Set the cake pan on top. With a pen or pencil, outline the circle that the pan makes. Cut the circle out of the paper and place inside the cake pan. Butter the parchment paper.

For the cake:

6 oz. semi-sweet chocolate chips

6 Tbsp. butter

¾ cup sugar

3 eggs

1 cup almond meal (ground almonds)- in the health section of the baking aisle

1 tsp. vanilla

½ cup unsweetened cocoa powder

Optional: Top the cooled cake with chocolate ganache*

Preheat the oven to 375 degrees.

Put some water (2-3 inches) in a medium saucepan and bring to a low boil (simmer). Place the chocolate and butter in a bowl that is big enough to sit over the top of the saucepan (and not touch the water). Place the bowl over the simmering water, and melt the chocolate and butter, stirring occasionally until smooth (if you use a steel bowl, you may need to use a towel to protect your hands from the heat while you stir).

Remove the bowl from over the heat and turn the heat off. Whisk the sugar into the chocolate mix to combine. Add the eggs and whisk until fully incorporated. Add the almond meal and vanilla, and whisk. Add the cocoa and whisk just until combined.

Bake 21-22 minutes. The top will form a thin crust. Cool on a rack for about 15 minutes. Invert onto a serving plate and peel the parchment paper off.

For the ganache:

1/2 cup heavy whipping cream

4 oz. semi-sweet chocolate chips

*To make the ganache:

Bring ½ cup whipping cream to a simmer in small saucepan over medium heat. Remove from heat. Add 4 oz. chocolate chips and whisk until smooth. Pour the ganache over the top of the cake and spread. Let it run down the sides a bit. Refrigerate the cake until the ganache is set, about 30-45 minutes.

Chocolate Cupcakes with Shiny Chocolate Ganache

Makes 18 cupcakes.

Follow the Yummy Chocolate Cake recipe for divine chocolate cupcake batter. Go further toward chocolate heaven and dip each cupcake in chocolate ganache. A worthwhile splurge? You be the judge.

Preheat the oven to 350 degrees.

Prepare the batter for the Yummy Chocolate Cake.

Spray the inside and top of a muffin tin well with Pam (so any cake over hang won't stick). Insert paper liners. Fill the liners with cake batter. Distribute the ¼ cup of chocolate chips among the cupcakes. Bake for about 16 minutes, or until a toothpick inserted in the center comes out without batter attached (moist crumbs are fine, even desired!). Try not to over-bake.

Let the cupcakes cool before frosting.

For the chocolate ganache frosting:

1 cup heavy whipping cream

1 cup semi-sweet chocolate chips

Put the chocolate chips in a medium bowl. Bring the cream to a simmer in a small pot over medium heat. Remove from the heat and pour the cream over the chocolate. Whisk until smooth.

One at a time, turn a cupcake upside down, dip the top in the ganache, and lift out with a swirling motion. Place one on your plate (get a tall glass of cold milk!) and enter chocolate bliss!

Yummy Chocolate Cake with Homemade Cream Cheese Icing

Serves 12 - 16.

You can prepare this cake in one bowl- and it may very well become your go-to chocolate cake favorite. Homemade chocolate cake with cream cheese icing... yup, sometimes you just have to go for it! Whenever I make this recipe, the entire kitchen smells like chocolate.

1¾ cups flour

¾ cup unsweetened cocoa

2 cups sugar

1 ½ tsp. baking soda

1 ½ tsp. baking powder

1 tsp. salt

1 cup skim milk

1/2 cup Canola oil

2 eggs

1 tsp. vanilla

1 cup boiling water

1 tsp. instant coffee or instant espresso

¼ cup semi-sweet chocolate chips

Preheat the oven to 350 degrees.

Spray two 9" cake pans with Pam.

Put the dry ingredients in a large bowl and stir to combine. Add the milk, oil, eggs, and vanilla. Beat with your electric mixer until well combined, about 2 minutes. Put the water in a small saucepan over high heat. Take it off the heat when it starts to boil and add the coffee. Stir to combine.

Stir the coffee and water mixture into the batter with a wooden spoon until the mixture is combined. Don't worry if it's thinner than other batters you've made. Pour the batter equally (as equally as you can!) into the two cake pans. Distribute the chocolate chips between the two pans-just scatter them, one by one.

Bake for 21-23 minutes, or until a toothpick inserted in the center comes out without batter attached (moist crumbs are fine, even desired!). I like to carefully switch the places of the pans about mid-way through the baking. Key in this recipe is not to overcook the cake! Let the cake cool before frosting.

Note that because the pans probably won't contain exactly equal batter amounts, if one toothpick test tells you it's time, take that cake out, and give the other one a minute at a time more, until the tester comes out without batter attached.

Cream Cheese Icing

8 oz. cream cheese at room temperature*

4 Tbsp. unsalted butter at room temperature*

3 cups powdered sugar

½ tsp. vanilla extract

Put the cream cheese, butter, and powdered sugar in a large bowl and mix with your electric mixer on medium speed, until the mixture is nice and smooth and looks like icing should! Add the vanilla and mix just long enough to incorporate.

*Who wants to wait for the butter or cream cheese to come to room temp?!

My trick is to use the microwave. For the butter, I leave it in its wax paper wrapping, and heat in small second increments, starting with 12 seconds (then 4), until soft. Do it slowly so the butter doesn't melt.

For the cream cheese, I take it out of the package, stand it sideways on a paper towel (not flat, 'cause you don't want the whole thing to stick to the paper towel), and microwave it for about 14 seconds. Feel it, do another 12 seconds, and continue with small second increments until it's soft.

To put the cake together:

Place one cooled cake (upside down) on your cake plate, frost the top of the cake. Place the other cake on top (right side up) and frost the top and the sides of the cake. Beauty!

Amazing Flourless Banana Bread

....

Yield: One loaf.

This banana bread is different from most because it contains ground almonds instead of flour (gluten-free!). It comes out amazingly delicious and moist, and it is one of those minutes-to-prepare recipes. Note that the shortbread jam cookie and fudge-y flourless chocolate cake recipes also use almond meal. It is a wonderful and increasingly popular alternative to flour.

I have developed a little trick to make it a one bowl recipe. I mash the bananas in the large bowl, push them to one side of the bowl, add the eggs and beat them on the empty side of the bowl. Then I mix the bananas and eggs together with a fork, add the remaining ingredients, and transfer to the loaf pan.

3 medium-large ripe bananas, mashed

2 eggs, beaten

2 cups almond meal/flour (usually in the health section of the baking aisle)

1 tsp. baking soda

¼ cup brown sugar

Optional: Add ¾ cup chocolate chips

Preheat the oven to 350 degrees.
Spray a standard size loaf pan with Pam.

Mash the bananas in a large bowl. Add the eggs and stir with a fork to combine. Add the remaining ingredients and stir just until well combined. Bake for 39 minutes. A toothpick should come out without batter attached. After the first 25 minutes, if the bread is looking like it's getting pretty brown, cover loosely with foil.

Note: If you would rather use all-purpose flour, just use regular sugar, bake for 36 minutes, and test as above for doneness. Since the texture of this bread is a little less delicate, consider add-ins such as ¾ cup walnuts- or a combination of chopped dried apricots and almonds, or dried cranberries and pistachio nuts.

Chocolate Toffee Pecan Pie

Serves 10.

This Chocolate Toffee Pecan Pie is beautiful and delicious. And, making a graham cracker crust is easier than a traditional pastry crust. It would be a great dessert for Thanksgiving, or any other time you want to share an indulgent dessert with friends! Just plan ahead a bit since the pie bakes for about 40 minutes.

One time I wanted to bring this out to the equestrian center where I volunteer, but I thought of it too late to allow for the baking time. So, I made mini chocolate pecan pies instead. I put graham cracker crust portions into a muffin tin sprayed with Pam, omitted the chocolate toffee bars in the recipe, gently spooned the filling into the crusts, and baked them until the filling was set (of course they took a fraction of the time to cook). The pies got rave reviews!

For the crust:

1 cup graham cracker crumbs (buy ones with as few, straightforward ingredients as you can)

4 Tbsp. butter melted

For the filling:

4 chocolate toffee bars, chopped (such as Heath bars)

4 eggs

1/2 cup sugar

½ tsp. salt

1 cup light corn syrup

1 Tbsp. butter, melted

1 tsp. vanilla

1 cup semi-sweet chocolate chips

1 cup pecan halves

Preheat the oven to 350 degrees.
Have a 9 inch pie plate ready to use.

Add the melted butter to the graham crackers in a medium bowl and mix with a spoon (I use a soup spoon from my flatware set) until all the crumbs are moistened. Pat the crust into your pie plate (it can go up the sides a bit) as evenly as possible. I like to pick some up with my fingers, put it in the pie plate, and pat- until I've used all the crumbs (and have a pretty even thickness throughout). Set the bowl aside- you can use it later. Bake the crust for 6 minutes and set aside.

Preheat the oven to 400.
Chop the toffee bars. Set aside.

In the same bowl you used for the crumbs, whisk the eggs together. Add the sugar, salt, corn syrup, butter, and vanilla. Whisk until well combined. Stir in the chocolate chips and pecans. Gently place the toffee pieces pretty evenly on the bottom of the pie crust and pour the filling on top. Put the pie in the oven and immediately reduce the temperature to 350. Cook for 38-40 minutes, or until the filling is set in the center. If the crust is pretty brown after about 25 minutes, place about three pieces of foil (folded lengthwise and bent to curve) on top of the crust. This will prevent over-browning.

Chocolate Chip Bread Pudding

....

Serves 12.

There are so many variations of bread puddings, many of them unnecessarily rich and cloyingly sweet! Though this version is much healthier than most, it is still utterly delicious and decadent tasting. It always gets rave reviews! Volunteer to bring dessert to a friend's house, and you'll see for yourself. You can go over the top and serve it with an easily made homemade caramel sauce (recipe below).

6 cups (packed down) good quality* challah bread or croissants (5-6 large), cut into cubes

½ cup semi-sweet chocolate chips, plus ¼ cup

3 eggs, lightly beaten

3 1/2 cups fat free evaporated milk

½ cup skim or 1% milk

3/4 cup fat free Greek yogurt (such as Fage or Oikos brand)

1 tsp. vanilla

¼ cup sugar

¼ cup brown sugar

Simple, pronounce-able ingredients (and not a paragraph long!)

Preheat the oven to 350 degrees.
Spray a 9x13 glass baking dish with Pam.

Place the bread cubes on a rimmed baking sheet and toast for 8 minutes (tossing after 5 minutes). Allow to cool for 5 minutes. Place the toasted bread cubes in the baking dish. Sprinkle evenly with ½ cup chocolate chips. Combine the remaining ingredients (except for the ¼ cup of chocolate chips) in a medium bowl with a whisk. Pour the mixture over the bread. Submerge all the bread cubes and allow them to soak for 15-30 minutes. Sprinkle with ¼ cup of chocolate chips and bake for about 40 minutes. The liquid should be absorbed and the bread pudding should look moist, not dry.

Variation with Homemade Caramel Sauce

Banana Bread Pudding with Homemade Caramel Sauce:

Increase the yogurt to 1 ¾ cups. And, instead of the chocolate in the recipe, after you have combined the egg mixture with a whisk, stir in 4 good sized ripe bananas (sliced), 1 tsp. cinnamon, and ½ tsp. cardamom (optional). Push the bananas down into the pudding before baking.

¾ cup packed dark brown sugar

¾ cup whipping cream

3 Tbsp. dark corn syrup

3 Tbsp. unsalted butter

½ tsp. vanilla

¼ tsp. salt

Bring the first 3 ingredients to a boil in a medium saucepan over medium heat, whisking until sugar dissolves. Boil caramel 5 minutes, whisking occasionally. Remove the pot from the heat. Whisk in the butter, vanilla and salt until smooth. Leftover sauce would be great over ice cream or frozen yogurt, or as a dip for apple slices!

"Food, like a loving touch or a glimpse of divine power, has that ability to comfort.

- Norman Kolpas

Grandma's Banana Cream Pie

Grandma's Banana Cream Pie

....

Serves 8.

Memories of dinner at Grandma's house include her pies. There was usually one pie waiting in the refrigerator, covered with wax paper, but, if more were coming for dinner, there were multiples! After we enjoyed a scrumptious meal, Grandma would whip the cream and top the pie(s) just before serving them. One afternoon, my husband and I sat with Grandma in her den, and recorded her oral recitation of the recipe on a piece of yellow paper, which I still have. True, this recipe uses a boxed pudding mix, but in her time that was common. The pie is delicious and it's just the way Grandma made it!

The recipe may look long on the page, but it's not hard. It's just my in-the-kitchen-with-you style.

Note: You do need to plan ahead for this one because the pie needs 3-4 hours in the refrigerator to cool before you can top it with the whipped cream.

For the crust:

1 cup graham cracker crumbs

3 Tbsp. butter, melted

For the filling:

1 large (4.6 oz.) package Jello brand "Cook 'N Serve" vanilla pudding mix (not instant)

2 ½ cups 2% milk

1 tsp. vanilla

4-5 good sized fairly ripe bananas, sliced into about ¼ inch thick circles (to be added when you assemble the pie)

For the whipped cream:

1 pint heavy whipping cream

2 Tbsp. sugar

1 tsp. vanilla

Preheat the oven to 350 degrees.
Spray a glass pie plate with Pam.
Have an electric mixer handy.

Procedure:

First, make the crust:

In a small bowl, combine the graham cracker crumbs and butter with a spoon (I use a soup spoon from my flatware set-just the right size). Stir and press down with the back of the spoon until the crumbs are fully moistened.

The way I like to line the pie plate is as follows:

Take some crust mix out with your fingers and place in the pie plate. Press down gently. Continue until you cover the bottom of the plate, trying to have about the same thickness of crumbs throughout. Then, use what's left to press some of the crust mixture up the sides of the plate. It will only go a little bit of the way up the sides. Bake for 10 minutes. Set aside to cool a bit.

Make the filling: Note that I like to start slicing the bananas in between stirring the pudding, but if you would rather wait until the pudding is done, that's o.k. You just might need to stir the pudding a few times to get it together (and incorporate the thin skin that might form on top).

Follow the box directions for making pudding, except use 2 ½ cups of milk instead of 3. I like stirring with a whisk. The pudding will thicken as it approaches a full boil. At this point, remove the pot from the heat. Add the vanilla, and stir to combine.

Assemble the pie:

Place a layer of bananas on the bottom of the crust. Feel free to overlap the holes with an extra banana slice. Spoon about half of the pudding over the bananas and spread to cover the bananas. Repeat with the remaining bananas and pudding.

Put the pie in the refrigerator to cool. You don't need to cover it at first. When it is cool, you can cover it with some plastic wrap.

To make the whipped cream:

Pour the cream, sugar, and vanilla into a medium size bowl. Mix with your electric mixer, starting on a slow speed to avoid splattering. When the mixture gets foamy, then switch to a high speed. Mix until the cream has begun to thicken. Keep going a bit and then check. It's done when it starts to look like whipped cream, and when, if you stop mixing and lift the beaters out of the cream, it leaves a soft peak.

If the cream stiffens and looks grainy, STOP! You're halfway to butter!

Note: You can make the whipped cream ahead of time, cover it with plastic wrap, and keep it in a steel bowl (it retains the cool) in the fridge 'til the pie is completely cooled and ready to top. Or, you can wait 'til you are ready to eat, whip the cream then, and top the cooled pie (a rubber spatula is a good tool for this). Enjoy!

Baby Key Lime Pies with a Gingersnap Crust

....

Makes 12 individual pies.

These pies are so cute, and they are just the right size. You can enjoy them perfectly tart just as they are, or with a small dollop of whipped cream or Mascarpone cheese (found near the cream cheese and sour cream at the grocery store) mixed with a touch of vanilla if you crave a little indulgence. While I am partial to using key limes for this recipe, I have made these with regular limes (about 6 good sized juicy ones) when key limes aren't available. Juicing takes less time, and the pies are still tasty (can see HELPING HAND for getting the most juice out of lemons and limes)!

12 store bought ginger snap cookies (it's not too hard to find ones with just a few straightforward ingredients)

2 eggs

1 14 oz. can sweetened condensed milk (I use Eagle brand)

1/2 cup fresh key lime juice (key limes are usually sold by the bag)

1/4 tsp. vanilla

Optional garnish: Small dollop of whipped cream (see Grandma's Banana Cream Pie recipe) or mascarpone cheese mixed with a touch of vanilla.

Preheat the oven to 325 degrees.

Line a muffin tin with paper cupcake liners (foil lined work best). Spray each liner with Pam.

Place a cookie (flat side up) in the bottom of each liner. In a large bowl, whisk (gently at first, to avoid sloshing) the eggs, condensed milk, lime juice, and vanilla together until very well mixed. Pour the mix as equally as you can into the muffin liners. Bake for about 15 minutes, until the pies are set in the middle. After you remove them from the oven, let them cool in the muffin tin for about 15 minutes, then place on a tray or plate and put in the fridge to allow them to cool completely.

Berries and Kiwi Fruit with Brown Sugar Vanilla Yogurt Sauce

....

Serves 6.

Sometimes, a light and refreshing dessert is just what you want. The yogurt sauce has just the right touch of sweet and the fruit combination is colorful, delicious, and loaded with nutrition. For breakfast, this sauce would be great over some healthy granola (low in fat, low in sugar) with some banana slices.

The fruit:

4 cups halved strawberries

1 pint blueberries or blackberries

3 kiwi, diced (can see HELPING HAND for peeling tip)

For the sauce:

1 cup plain, nonfat Greek yogurt

¼ tsp. cinnamon

½ tsp. vanilla

1 ½ Tbsp, brown sugar

Mix the yogurt, cinnamon, vanilla, and brown sugar together in a medium bowl with a whisk. Set aside.

Prepare the fruit and gently mix together in a serving bowl. To dry the berries after rinsing, I like to lay out a clean kitchen towel, pour the rinsed fruit over the towel, and gently roll a paper towel over the fruit. Serve the fruit into individual dishes and dress with some of the yum yogurt sauce. Enjoy!

Golden Pear Crisp

....

Serves 8.

Pears are delicious by themselves, but a little indulgence - picture warm crisp with vanilla ice cream or frozen yogurt - never hurts. This recipe is wonderful and easy. Its aroma will bathe your olfactories with a buttery goodness that makes your mouth water!

6 medium Anjou pears* (the green ones), peeled and cut into chunks

½ tsp. cinnamon

¼ tsp. nutmeg

1 1/2 Tbsp. brown sugar

Juice from ½ small lemon

For the topping:

1/4 cup flour

¼ cup oats

5 tbsp. butter, cut into 1 inch cubes

2 Tbsp. brown sugar

* You want the pears to be firm, but not too hard.

Preheat the oven to 375 degrees. Spray a pie plate with Pam.

Put the pears, spices, and sugar in a large bowl. Squeeze the lemon (cut side up, so you can catch any seeds in your hand) over the pears and toss to combine. Put the mix in your pie plate.

Just wipe the bowl dry with a paper towel and put the flour, oats, butter and brown sugar in the bowl. Mix together with your fingers. When the mixture is crumbly (kind of resembles small peas), sprinkle the crumbs pretty evenly over the top of the fruit. Bake for about 30-45 minutes or until bubbly and the top is turning golden. Yum!

Homemade Cinnamon Applesauce

....

Serves 4.

Applesauce just isn't at its best when it comes from a jar. How can it beat one made easily at home from fresh chopped apples, water, and a touch of cinnamon? This is super easy to make and pretty delicious warm.

4 medium apples of your choosing (I prefer Fuji, Honey Crisp, or Golden delicious), cored and cut into chunks

½ cup water or apple juice (no sugar added)

1/2 tsp. cinnamon

Put the apples and water or juice in a medium saucepan. Bring to a boil. Reduce to a simmer and cover. Cook until the apples are soft, about 15 minutes. Mash with a potato masher until the applesauce is the consistency that you like. Stir in the cinnamon. Enjoy warm or cold.

Blackberry Raspberry Party

....

Serves 8.

There is nothing quite like walking out to our orchard in Hood River, Oregon, and picking the berries to be used in this summer treat. Wherever you get your berries, though, the aroma in your kitchen as your crumble bakes will radiate goodness. And, if you want to enjoy the splendor of two other wonderful summertime fruits, see below for the Peach Blueberry Crumble adaptation.

Fruit mix:

18 oz. fresh blackberries

12 oz. fresh raspberries

2 golden delicious apples, peeled and chopped

1 ½ tsp. sugar

1 Tbsp. fresh lemon juice

1 Tbsp. flour

Topping:

½ cup flour

1/3 cup brown sugar

6 Tbsp. butter, cut into cubes

Preheat the oven to 350 degrees.
Have a glass pie plate or shallow baking dish handy.

Combine the fruit, sugar, lemon juice and flour in a large bowl and transfer to your pie plate. For the topping, combine the flour and sugar in a small bowl. Incorporate the butter, either with a fork, or by crumbling with your fingers, until the mixture is crumbly (kind of resembles small peas). Cover the fruit mix with the flour mixture and bake for 35-40 minutes, or until bubbling and golden. Delish!

Variation: To make an awesome **Peach Blueberry Crumble** for 6, combine 4 pretty large, ripe peaches (sliced), 1 pint fresh blueberries, and 1 Tbsp. flour in a large bowl. Transfer to a 11x7 baking dish. In the same bowl, combine ¼ cup flour, 3 Tbsp. oats, 1/3 cup brown sugar, ¼ tsp. cinnamon, and 1/8 tsp. nutmeg. Add 3 Tbsp. butter (cut into cubes) and incorporate as directed above. Proceed as in above recipe.

A HELPING HAND

This section is here as an extra guide for you. The first part offers tips of a general nature and the second part offers a list, in alphabetical order, of items in my recipes that you might want a little extra help with.

Let your food be your medicine and your medicine be your food.

- Hippocrates

IN GENERAL

Sign up for a knife skills class if you can. A place that offers cooking classes will probably offer a knife skills class as well.

Food Safety -

When you have touched raw chicken, meat, or fish, always wash your hands before going on to something else.

The same applies to utensils, cutting boards, plates, etc. If they have come in contact with raw chicken, meat or fish, put them in the sink for later washing.

Don't use plastic containers or plastic wrap when heating food in the microwave. You don't want chemicals to be released into the food. Use glass containers instead, and cover the food with a paper towel instead of plastic wrap.

Boiling vs Simmering -

Think of it like this: boiling is active, vigorous bubbling. A simmer is boiling, but way chilled out…a gentle boil.

Chopped vs Diced vs Minced -

When I say chopped, I mean you don't have to cut the pieces too small—just kind of bite sized. Diced is pretty small, maybe half the size of "chopped." Minced is really small (a good example is mincing garlic).

Measuring -

To measure dry ingredients, use standard dry measuring cups.

To measure liquids, use standard liquid measuring cups with a pouring spout. Place the cup on a level surface and check at eye level.

Standard measuring spoons are used for both dry and liquid measures.

When measuring flour, you don't want it to be really packed into the measuring cup. Kind of tilt the bag of flour so the flour isn't as compact, and then measure the amount you need.

With regard to *eggs* in the recipes, assume large size.

With regard to *butter* in the recipes, assume unsalted.

With regard to *brown sugar* in the recipes, either light or dark is okay. The dark brown sugar just has more molasses in it.
When measuring brown sugar for recipes in the book, assume that you should pack it down into the measuring cup.

When preparing a *menu*, if you need one ingredient (e.g. garlic) for more than one recipe, chop enough one time, so you won't have to repeat the process for each recipe!

If you are making something, say, latkes (potato pancakes), or a dish that you need to keep warm until the rest of your meal is ready, you can generally keep it in a 200 degree oven.

When you need to *stir* or *whisk* something together, place a damp kitchen towel under the bowl to help the bowl stay put.

Tip for drying blueberries, cherry tomatoes, or similar fruits before using them: I like to lay out a clean kitchen towel. Then, rinse the fruit in a colander and give it a little shake over the sink to get rid of excess water. Gently pour the fruit over the towel. If the towel is big enough, fold the edges over and gently roll the towel over the top of the fruit. If the towel isn't big enough, use a paper towel to cover the fruit and gently roll that over the fruit. Voila! Clean, dry fruit ready to use.

ACORN SQUASH

Selecting Acorn Squash

Choose squash that are heavy for their size, and are a little dull in color (as opposed to shiny and very dark green, which may not be ripe yet), with some orange coloring on the skin. Avoid any blemishes or moldy spots. The hard skin of a winter squash protects the flesh, so it can be stored longer than the familiar yellow (crook-necked) squash. It doesn't need refrigeration

AVOCADO

Selecting and Preparing Avocados

When selecting an avocado, gently squeeze the fruit in the palm of your hand. Ripe, ready-to-eat fruit will be firm yet will yield to gentle pressure. Pick one without blemishes or sunken areas.

To peel the avocado, cut it lengthwise around the seed, and rotate the halves to separate. Remove the seed by sliding the tip of a spoon gently underneath and lifting out. Then, either just scoop out the avocado meat with a spoon, or, if you want slices, quarter the avocado and peel the skin off with your fingers. Then slice.

If you are making guacamole, but not going to eat right away, keep the avocado pit and place it inside your mixed guacamole. That will reduce browning while the guac waits to be consumed!

If you are preparing sliced avocados a little ahead of time, sprinkle the cut surfaces with lemon or lime juice to keep them from turning brown.

To ripen an avocado, place the fruit in a plain brown paper bag or on the window sill. If the avocado is already ripe, you can store it in the fridge for a few days.

BASIL

How to "chiffonade" Basil

Lay the basil leaves one on top of the other in a stack. Roll them lengthwise into a log shape. After you have a tight roll, slice crosswise into thin slices and you'll end up with beautiful long strands of basil.

BEETS

Selecting and Preparing Beets

Beets are available year round but are best from late spring through late fall. Look for beets with good color that are firm and heavy for their size. They should have smooth skin with no splits, and they should not be sprouting. If leaves are attached they should look fresh and bright colored.

Go for golf ball size. Really big ones can be wood-y. They will also take longer to cook.

When preparing to use beets, scrub thoroughly.

Beet greens will keep 3 or 4 days in the fridge. Cut off the leaves about 1" from the beet root, and place in a plastic bag in the refrigerator.

A simple way to enjoy beet greens:

Wash the beet greens in a sink filled with cold water. Let them drain some in a colander, but you want them to stay a little wet. Roughly chop the greens. Put them in a large pot, cover, and cook over medium heat until wilted. No need to add water because the moisture from the washed leaves will be enough. They cook pretty fast, and they wilt down a LOT, just like spinach. When cooked, put the beet greens in your serving bowl, and season with a tad of butter, and salt and pepper to taste. Simple, good food!

I also love these on a sandwich, as you would use lettuce.

BOK CHOY

Selecting and Preparing Bok Choy

Look for firm, pure white stalks and dark green leaves without brown spots. Before using, cut off the root end and pull off any limp or discolored leaves. Separate the leaves while holding the bok choy under running water until all visible dirt has been washed away.

Note that if you are using full size bok choy (as opposed to baby bok choy), wash as above, and separate the leaves from the stalks because the stalks take longer to cook. Cut or tear the leaves, and cut the stalks into small slices along the diagonal.

BRUSSELS SPROUTS

Selecting and Preparing Brussels Sprouts

Peak season for these is fall 'til early spring. Look for sprouts that are firm, compact, and vivid green. Avoid ones with yellowed or wilted leaves, and leaves with holes in them. It's optimal to choose sprouts of similar size, so they will cook evenly.

Wash them well under running water.

BUTTERNUT SQUASH

Selecting and Preparing Butternut Squash for Roasting

Butternut squash is a winter variety, with a peak season of early fall through winter. It is usually pear shaped and its color ranges from yellow to light tan. A ripe squash should feel heavy for its size. The skin should be free of cuts or punctures, and brown spots can indicate frostbite. Those with wider necks will have more flesh.

The most important thing to consider when cutting butternut squash is to keep the pieces you are working with as stable as possible. To prepare for roasting, cut the ends off of the squash. Use a good vegetable peeler to peel off the outer layer. Stand the peeled squash upright on a cutting board. It shouldn't wobble. Make one long cut, down the middle from the top to bottom, with a heavy chef's knife. To help with the cutting you can use a rubber mallet to gently tap on the ends of the knife to help push the knife down through the squash.

Use a metal spoon to scrape out the seeds and the stringy pulp from the squash cavity. Lay the squash halves, cut side down on the cutting board for stability. Cut the squash into slices or cubes, whatever you need.

CAULIFLOWER

Selecting and Preparing Cauliflower

Look for white, unblemished flower clusters with green, non-wilted leaves. To prepare for a recipe using florets, remove the outer leaves by slicing through the stem between the head of the cauliflower and the leaves with a chef's knife. Cut around the core with a paring knife (smaller than a chef's knife). Remove and discard the core. Break the head into florets, using a knife if necessary.

CHICKEN

How to Prep Chicken Breasts
(for any recipe using boneless skinless breasts)

Take out your knife and cutting board or plastic cutting sheet (I prefer these). Take a piece of chicken out of the package. Cut away any fat or tendon (basically, any of the stuff that doesn't look like the rest of the chicken). After you have all the chicken pieces nice and "cleaned," rinse under cool water and pat dry with a paper towel. Now, you're ready to go!

How to Make a Plain Sautéed Chicken Breast

If you ever want to make plain sautéed chicken to add to a salad, top with some roasted veggies, etc., here's how: Prep the boneless skinless breasts. Season the chicken on one side with a small pinch of Kosher salt and a sprinkle of pepper. Heat the pan over medium heat. Add 1 Tbsp. olive oil. Add the chicken, seasoned side down. Season the side facing you. Cook on medium heat until the chicken starts to turn golden (about 6-8 minutes or so). Flip and cook for another 6 to 8 minutes or so (depending on the thickness of the chicken). Test for doneness with the fork and knife technique described below. You really want to try not overcook, or the breast might end up being dry.

How to Make Plain Poached Chicken

Prep the chicken (only you don't need to pat them dry). Put the breasts into a saucepan and add water to a little more than cover them. Bring to a boil, turn down the heat to a gentle boil (simmer) and let them cook, uncovered, for about 15 minutes. When the chicken is done-it should no longer be pink in the middle- just set the breasts out on your cutting board or plastic cutting sheet to cool a bit.

How to Tell When Chicken is Done

This is not for the whole roasted chicken (see that recipe).

A chicken breast is done when no longer pink in the middle. To test, you can take a fork and a knife with a pointy tip and gently make a cut through the thickest part of a piece. If it's no longer pink, it's ready to eat!

If you have pieces that are not as thick as some, they'll cook a bit more quickly. So if you are cooking them on the stove top, and they are done first, you can go ahead and take them off the heat while you finish the rest. That way, they won't get dry from cooking too long.

CELERY ROOT

Selecting and Preparing Celeriac (Celery Root)

Look for firm, heavy roots that are compact and brown in color. Stay away from those with a greenish tinge, and ones that have slime at the bottom of the root. Check the ribs (the familiar looking celery!) at the top of the root. They should be small, supple and plentiful. It's an old root if they are large, stiff and hollow.

The root can look a little intimidating, but to peel before using, slice off one end and then the other end, giving you a flat top and bottom. Set it on the cutting board and cut the peel off with a knife, from top to bottom, all the way around. Removing the outer part will reveal the pearly white core. If you have extra, try grating it into a salad- very tasty!

EGGPLANT

Peeling an Eggplant

Slice off both ends of the eggplant. Now you can stand it up tall on its flat bottom. Take your knife and slice down lengthwise, all the way around. If you don't get every bit of skin off, it's not a big deal. It'll be fine that way.

Note: Japanese eggplants (those long, skinny, lighter purple ones) don't need to be peeled.

EGGS

Cracking an Egg

Don't crack an egg on the rim of a bowl because you'll be running the risk of getting bits of shell in it. Rather, take the egg in your hand, and using an up and down wrist motion, gently tap on the counter until there is a small dent in the shell. Then, with your thumbs on the opposite sides of the dent, gently pull apart the shells. Drop the egg in the small bowl you have set aside for that purpose.

Separating Eggs

Have a bowl set out near you (glass or ceramic work best since they are sturdy). Choose the freshest eggs possible; they separate more easily than older eggs.

Give the egg a good hit at its midpoint, against the inside of the bowl. Place your thumbs on either side of the dent and split the egg shell into 2 halves, allowing the yolk to remain in one shell half. Egg white will dribble out, so be sure to do this over your bowl.

Over the bowl, gently transfer the yolk back and forth between the two halves, allowing the egg white to drop into the bowl but keeping the egg yolk in the shell.

Once all the white part of the egg is in the bowl, you can discard the shell and yolk or put the yolk into a separate container for later use.

If, by chance, you get bits of eggshell into the bowl:

Use a large piece of broken shell to scoop it out. It acts like a magnet to help you fish out the smaller piece!

Before you add an egg to a bowl with other ingredients:

Just keep in mind that it's always safer to break the egg(s) into a separate container first. That way, if the egg isn't good (e.g. has specks of blood), or if a small piece of eggshell falls into the bowl, you can easily remove it.

How to Make Hard Boiled Eggs

Place the eggs in a saucepan and cover with cold water by an inch or so. Bring to a boil. Lower the heat to a slower boil and cook for 15 minutes. Move to the sink and pour the water out of the saucepan. Refill the pot with cold water, crack the eggs, and peel under a stream of cold water.

FENNEL

Selecting and Preparing Fennel

Look for whitish or pale green bulbs, without signs of splitting or bruising. The stalks and leaves should be green, and have no flowering buds (this means it's old).

Note that all parts of the fennel are edible - the bulb, the stalks, and the feathery leaves called fronds. Cut the stalks away from the bulb a little above where they meet. Cut the bulb in half vertically, slice the base off, and rinse it with water before proceeding to cut it further. It is best to slice it vertically. You can cut the stalks just as you would stalks of celery. The fronds can be used as an herb in salads, or as you like.

FIGS

Selecting and Storing Figs

Figs are at their peak when harvested and don't continue to ripen after they're picked. So, try to buy figs only a day or two before you plan to eat them. Look for figs that are tender to the touch and have a sweet fragrance. Since they are fragile, carefully touch each before you buy to make sure they haven't become too soft, and thus over-ripe.

If they aren't going to be consumed right away, they should be refrigerated, but are best enjoyed at room temperature.

FISH

How to Tell When Fish is Done

Just take a fork and a knife with a pointed tip and gently slice through the thickest part. Hold the knife leaning into the side of the fish a bit, so that you can get a peek almost through to the bottom. What you should see is that the fish doesn't look raw anymore. Also, when the fish is done, it will have milky white juices and it will flake easily.

As you get used to cooking fish, you'll be ready to aim for the perfect finish-that is, don't wait until it's totally cooked. If it looks like it's basically there, you can take it out of the oven or off the stove, and cover with foil. It will cook a bit more on its own.

GARLIC

Peeling Garlic Cloves

I'm all the about the whack method: Set the flat side of a wide blade knife on the garlic clove, and give it a whack! The peel will practically come right off.

Roasting Garlic

Preheat the oven to 400. Leave the paper-y skin on the garlic and cut off about ½ inch of the pointed top of the head, so that most of the cloves are exposed. Place the garlic in some foil, drizzle with ½ tsp. olive oil, and seal the foil like a pouch. Place in the oven for about 30-35 minutes. When the garlic is cool enough to handle, you can just squeeze the delicious, mellow-flavored garlic out. Spread on fresh baguette slices, top a pizza, add to a salad, or use any other way you think sounds good!

JICAMA

Selecting and Preparing Jicama

Jicama is a Mexican root vegetable in the potato family that is super crunchy and juicy. Great for snacking! It's covered with an inedible light-brown or gray skin, and ranges in size from little to huge!

Look for jicama with a thin skin (thick means it's old), and without cracks or bruises. You can peel as you would a potato, and remove all of the stringy parts of the outer shell. Lots of people like to eat jicama sticks sprinkled with lime juice and a little salt (with some cayenne pepper for a kick!).

KALE

Selecting Kale

Look for kale with unwilted, deeply colored leaves and moist, hardy stems. Avoid those with browning, yellowing or small holes. Kale with smaller-sized leaves will be more tender and have a more mild flavor than those with larger leaves.

KIWI

Peeling a Kiwi

Peelers are too rough for this fruit. You can just slice off the ends and peel the fuzzy skin off with a paring knife OR you can slice the kiwi in half and insert a small spoon between the skin and flesh of the fruit (bottom of the spoon up against the skin) and move the spoon gently around the fruit, separating the skin from the fruit.

LEMONS and LIMES

Extracting the Most Juice

First, try and choose fruit that feels like it would be juicy. Also, note that room temperature fruit will yield more juice.

A few tricks:

Cut the fruit lengthwise instead of along the equator. Before slicing the lemon or lime, microwave the fruit for 20-30 seconds. As the microwave heats the fruit from the inside out, the juice capsules burst within the fruit. Once the fruit has cooled enough to handle, slice it open and juice as normal.

Or, roll the lemon or lime on the countertop while applying gentle pressure with the heel of your hand.

If you're convinced there's still juice to be had, try twisting the citrus segments around a fork. The tines will help to break open any remaining bits of pulp.

MANGO

Selecting, Peeling and Cutting a Mango

Choose a mango that is brightly colored- either red, yellow, or orange, depending on the variety. It should have a fruity and sweet aroma, and be somewhat firm, but yield slightly to the touch. Avoid mangoes with soft spots.
Since the shape of a mango is odd and the flesh of the mango is pretty slippery, a few tips might help.

A couple of ways to go:

Cut a little slice off the ends of the mango. Stand it up on your cutting board/sheet.

Slice the skin off the mango, top to bottom, turning the fruit as you go, until all the peel is gone. Cut the flat sides of the flesh (trying to get close to the seed so that you get all the flesh). Cut off the rounded ends, and prepare as you wish.

OR

With the peel on the fruit, slice off the top and bottom of the fruit (the flat sides, not the tips). Get as close to the flat seed as possible.

Cut a tic-tac-toe pattern into the flesh of the fruit (vertical lines, about an inch apart, and then horizontal lines, about an inch apart). Cut to, but not through, the skin.

Holding the edges of one half of the fruit in your hands, press the skin with your thumbs to turn the slice inside out. Bite size chunks of fruit will extend from the skin, ready for you to scoop off with a spoon.

Slice off the rounded ends and slice the fruit out of those sections.

NUTS

How to Toast Nuts (almonds, pecans, you name it!)

Heat a small skillet over medium heat. Add the nuts. Stir every so often. Once you start to smell them and they are beginning to take on a little color, they are ready.

TRY REALLY HARD not to do what I have done countless times, which is to get involved in something else while they are toasting. I'm way too familiar with the quick dash outside to the trash can so that I can rid the kitchen of the offending smell of burnt nuts.

Another way to go:

Preheat the oven to 375 and put the nuts on a cookie sheet. Cook for about 6-8 minutes, tossing once. Once you start to smell them and they are beginning to take on a little color, they are ready.

REMEMBER THIS: after the nuts are toasted, transfer them from the cookie sheet to a plate in order to stop the cooking process.

How to Toast Pine Nuts

Toasting pine nuts gives them roasted flavor, browns them, and makes them firmer, too. It's easiest to do in a dry skillet over medium-low heat. Shake the skillet frequently to ensure even browning. The pine nuts are small and full of rich oil, and will burn quickly if you don't watch carefully. When the nuts are fragrant and browned, take the pan off the heat. Transfer the pine nuts to a plate to cool.

How to Chop Nuts

I like to use a sharp chef's knife to do the job. First, gather the nuts in a circle slightly smaller than the length of the knife's blade. Hold the knife, place your other hand over the top of the tip of the knife. Rock the blade back and forth, rotating it around the circle with a firm stroke. Periodically stop and reposition any nuts that have shifted outside of the circle. Continue chopping in this fashion until the nuts are the size you want.

ONIONS

Chopping an Onion (courtesy of Bon Appetit!)

1. Cut a small bit off the top of the onion to create a flat surface. This will ensure that the onion stays put during slicing.

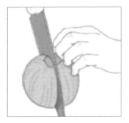

2. Position the onion on the flat end and halve it through the root end. Peel off and discard the onion skin.

3. Arrange one onion half on a cutting board, flat side down. Make evenly spaced vertical cuts in the onion, slicing downward toward the cutting board and stopping just short of the root end.

4. Position the knife blade parallel to the cutting board. Make evenly spaced horizontal cuts in the onion, again stopping just short of the root end.

5. Slice the onion across the vertical cuts, letting the diced pieces fall away. Repeat with the second half of the onion.

OKRA

Selecting and Preparing Okra

Look for young, green, tender pods no more than 4 inches long. Larger pods tend to be tough. Cut off a small piece from both the stalk and tip of each pod. If the pods are very "fuzzy," rub them lightly with a kitchen towel to remove some of the unwanted fuzz. Wash under cold water, and use whole or sliced thickly.

PARSLEY

Preparing Parsley

Remove the stems. Wash the parsley, trying to keep the bunch more or less intact (easier to chop that way). Squeeze dry before chopping, dicing, whatever.

Note that if the parsley is particularly gritty with dirt, the best thing to do is rinse it, then set it in a large bowl of water for a bit so the dirt can settle to the bottom. Lift the parsley out and rinse out the dirty water. Repeat until the water has no grit or dirt, and you will be good to go.

PARSNIPS

Selecting and Preparing Parsnips

Similar in look to carrots, parsnips have ivory colored skin and a unique, somewhat nutty flavor. Look for parsnips that are very firm, with no blemishes or cracks. Smaller parsnips tend to be sweeter. Large/thick ones tend to have woody, bitter cores. Cut off the stem end and any straggling roots. Peel before using if you like.

PEPPERS

Seeding Hot Peppers (e.g. jalapeno, Serrano)

FIRST, a word about touching hot peppers: be careful not to touch the pepper and then touch your mouth or eyes! I always rinse my hands after I seed and cut the peppers.

Cut off the top of the pepper and discard. Slice the pepper down the middle, lengthwise. Then, slice the pepper into quarters. Scrape the seeds from each quarter with your knife.

RUTABAGAS

Selecting and Preparing Rutabagas

Rutabagas resemble turnips, only with yellow-orange flesh. Choose rutabagas that are on the smaller side, firm, fresh looking, heavy for their size, and smooth, with little or no cuts or punctures.

The best way to peel a rutabaga: Wash it to remove any dirt. Slice the ends off and trim each side to create a rutabaga block. It will then be easy to peel the rest of the rutabaga (use a paring knife) as you are slicing it up.

SNOW PEAS

Selecting and Preparing Snow Peas

Look for dark green peas that do not appear dry or cracked. To trim them, just break off the stem end, and pull the string away from the pod.

STRAWBERRIES

Selecting and Storing Strawberries

When you buy strawberries, look for firm, fragrant ones. Before you eat or store them, pick out any soft or yucky looking ones. Don't remove the green caps or wash the berries until you are ready to eat them because moisture is the enemy! Also, try to use the berries as soon as possible since strawberries don't continue to ripen after they are picked.

A great way to make strawberries last: Pick out any soft or yucky looking ones, and, without washing the berries, refrigerate them in a sealed glass jar. They just last longer this way!

SUGAR SNAP PEAS

How to String Sugar Snap Peas

Sugar snap peas have strings that should be removed before eating. To do this, pinch the very tip of the pea, getting hold of the string. Pull the string up the straightest side toward the stem end; pinch off the stem end and continue pulling until there is no more string.

SWISS CHARD

Selecting and Preparing Swiss Chard

Swiss Chard is available year round, but has a peak season of June through August. The stalks come in a variety of colors-red, yellow, and white (white being the most tender). The fan-like leaves can be either smooth or curly. Look for chard with leaves that are vivid green in color, without any browning or yellowing. The leaves also should not be wilted or have tiny holes. The stalks should look crisp and be unblemished.

To prepare, rinse the chard under cold running water. To separate the leaves from the stalks, fold the chard leaf in half and cut off the stalk. For ease of prep, you can stack the leaves before cutting into the size pieces you desire. The stalks take longer to cook, so most recipes will start with them. You can just cut them into about 1 inch slices, as you would celery (discard the bottom inch or so).

TOMATOES

How to Seed Tomatoes

It's easiest to just cut the tomatoes in half crosswise and, over the sink, kind of work your thumbs into each side of the tomato half, trying to loosen the seeds. Then, holding the tomato in one hand, with the cut side facing the sink, shake downward a few times. This will get most of the liquid and seeds out.

TURNIPS

Selecting and Preparing Turnips

Select small , smooth skinned turnips that are heavy for their size. If the tops are attached, they should be fresh, green, and crisp (not yellow or wilted). Avoid turnips that are soft or have brown spots. Peel the turnip as you would a potato. Or, since some have a wax coating, cut off the top and bottom to create two flat surfaces. Set the turnip down flat on your cutting board and either run a vegetable peeler along the sides of the turnip or use a paring knife (while holding the turnip flat on the cutting board).

If the turnips are young and small (golf ball sized), they don't need to be peeled.

"TO YOUR HEALTH" QUICK TIPS

First and foremost, a great "rule of thumb" and my philosophy when buying things from the store:

Don't buy food with a paragraph of ingredients -

- some of which are even hard to pronounce. If you can't pronounce it or visualize it in an organic form, it's probably best not to ingest it!

And, since the packaged, processed food is altered from its natural state for convenience and extended shelf life, it makes you think…

Go organic whenever you can!

Why?

One of the best reasons to eat organic food is that it tastes great! If you were to stage a blindfold test, I bet you would choose the organic foods based on taste alone.

Organically grown foods contain a higher percentage of nutrients, antioxidants, natural vitamins (such as C, beta carotene and B), and minerals (such as chromium, selenium, calcium, boron, lithium, and magnesium) in their natural, easily-assimilated form.

And, there are many other reasons: no chemicals, preservatives, heavy metal residues, antibiotics (that can cause allergic reactions or intolerance), or hormones.

Eat lots of fresh fruits and vegetables, whole grains, seeds, and nuts.

Why?

Well, fruits and veggies add color (generally the darker and more colorful a fruit or vegetable is, the higher it will be in vitamins, minerals, and antioxidants), texture, and appeal to your plate. They are naturally low in calories and add water and fiber to your diet. They also help your body function and may reduce your risk of many diseases, including heart disease, high blood pressure, diabetes, and cancer. Good stuff!

The healthiest kinds of grains are **whole grains**. They add texture and flavor to your diet and they are a great source of fiber and other important nutrients.

Nuts and seeds -

Are excellent sources of protein. And, they have lots of other benefits, such as vitamins, minerals, fiber, enzymes, and healthy fats! Some great choices include almonds, cashews, flaxseeds, pumpkin seeds, sesame seeds, sunflower seeds, and walnuts.

Eat seasonally.

That is, try to focus your meals on fruits and vegetables that are fresh and in season. Your body and your wallet will benefit!

EXPAND YOUR REPERTOIRE

If you like spinach -

Try kale, Swiss chard, mustard greens, collard greens, beet greens, and broccoli rabe. They can all be sautéed. Just heat a little olive oil in a skillet over medium heat, add a few chopped garlic cloves and the greens (trimmed and roughly torn), salt, and pepper. Cook until tender, stirring occasionally.

If you like carrots -

Try turnips, rutabagas, sweet potatoes, parsnips, beets (wrap these in foil; they take about 45 minutes to cook, depending on their size), acorn squash, delicata squash, buttercup squash, and butternut squash. These are all very tasty when roasted with a little olive oil, salt, and pepper until tender.

If you like broccoli -

Try broccolini, Brussels sprouts, cauliflower, and fennel. These are also great when roasted as above.

Have fun at a Farmer's Market.

Sampling all those fresh fruits and veggies is fun and inspiring. You'll get hooked!

Drink Green Tea.

Why?

It's about the process. Green tea leaves are steamed (not made from fermented leaves), which prevents the powerful antioxidant compound EGCG from being oxidized. EGCG has been shown to inhibit cancer cell growth, reduce the risk of heart disease and stroke, and even prevent tooth decay. It does have caffeine, but less than coffee!

Avoid sugar substitutes

like NutraSweet and Equal. They are made with Aspartame, and that isn't good for you.

IF YOU'RE TRYING TO LOSE WEIGHT

Try these suggestions:

Decrease the amount of carbohydrates that you consume. Of course, not all carbs are created equal. Simple carbs, like sugar, honey, and refined flour are not as good for you as complex carbs, such as legumes, whole grains, and leafy vegetables. (What are legumes, anyway? They are a class of vegetables that include beans, peas, and lentils. And, they're actually among the most versatile and nutritious foods around!)

Eat from smaller plates and bowls. Research has actually shown that this makes a difference.

Eat more slowly.

Eat an apple or other high fiber, low calorie fruit or veggie before your meal.

Try whole grain mustard on your sandwiches instead of mayo. Not only is the flavor rich, but mustard seeds are a good source of the antioxidant selenium.

When baking cake or muffins from a recipe that calls for a lot of oil or butter, try substituting half (or 2/3) of the fat called for with a sweet puree like applesauce, pumpkin, or mashed bananas. Of course, an added bonus is that you get more fruits and veggies!

I find that you can almost always use less sugar than what is called for in traditional baked good recipes.

In recipes that call for sour cream, try using low or non-fat Greek yogurt instead. It has a rich taste and texture, and a bunch of protein!

Of course, sodas are not a friend in general, but particularly if you are trying to lose weight. Try adding a splash of your favorite juice, like orange, pomegranate, or cranberry to some sparkling water. One of my favorites is sparkling water with fresh lime juice and some crushed mint. Quintessentially refreshing!

"Tell me what you eat, I'll tell you who you are."

- Anthelme Brillat-Savarin

KITCHEN TOOLS

Dry measure measuring cups (stainless steel will last a long time, so it's worth spending a little bit more)

Liquid measuring cup

Measuring spoons

A timer— I love mine, and use it all the time!

Cutting board or thin plastic cutting sheets (I use these - they're light, easy, and dishwasher friendly)

Wire whisk

Potato masher

Can opener

Vegetable peeler

Grater

Salad spinner

Wooden spoons

Small pastry brush

Knives (particularly a good 8" chef's knife)

Parchment paper

Set of different sized steel mixing bowls (you'll use these tons - I have had mine for over 30 years and use them almost every day!)

Basic set of pots and pans:

3 sizes of skillets/fry pans - small, medium and large (you'll probably use a 12 inch a lot)

2 sizes of saucepans - a 2 qt. and a 3 qt.

A saucepan/stockpot large enough to hold a whole chicken - 8 or 10 qt.

Cookie sheet

Rimmed baking sheet

Muffin tin

9 x 5" Standard loaf pan (e.g. for banana bread)

Two 9" round cake pans

8 or 9" square baking pan (perfect for brownies!)

11 x 7" glass baking dish (Pyrex is great)

9 x 13" glass baking dish (Pyrex is great)

9" glass pie plate (Pyrex is great)

A large roasting pan (with cover)

Hand held electric mixer

Blender (e.g. for smoothie)

Ice cream scoop with a release lever

Metal Spatula

Flexible spatula (for scraping bowls)

Pot holder

Toothpicks

Kitchen twine/string (e.g. for tying chicken drumsticks together)

Meat thermometer

Metal cooling rack (e.g. for cooling cookies)

Colander (e.g. for draining spaghetti)

Pizza pan (or, you could use a rimmed baking sheet for the pizza-so what if your pizza isn't round!)

You need a food processor to make Classic Hummus and Spiced Falafel Spread. It would come in handy for Latkes and the Raw Beet Salad as well.

Food is our common ground, a universal experience.

— James Beard

ELLI'S PANTRY - GREAT BUILDING BLOCKS

Some Key Spices:

Salt

Kosher salt

Pepper

Garlic powder

Onion powder

Chili powder

Cumin

Dried oregano

Paprika

Ground mustard

Cayenne pepper / red chili flakes (if you like heat)

Cinnamon

Ground ginger

Nutmeg

Other Items That Are Handy To Have On Hand:

Olive oil

Original "Pam"

Worcestershire sauce

Balsamic vinegar*

Red wine Vinegar

Dijon mustard

Whole Grain mustard

Canola oil

Chicken and/or vegetable broth (99% fat free is pretty easy find)

Canned beans (with few added ingredients)

Honey

Nuts (e.g. walnuts, pecans, almonds)

Fresh garlic

Lemons, limes

*A note about Balsamic vinegar:

While for making salad dressings and sauces, it's fine to use a mid-grade, it is well worth the money to buy a truly good Balsamic vinegar. It is surprisingly expensive (the longer it has been aged, the more expensive it is), but a few drops go a long way.

Most grocery store "balsamic" vinegars are red wine vinegar with caramel coloring. The real thing is made primarily of grape must.

So, when the balsamic is one of the stars in a dish, like drizzling over cooked vegetables (try it over sliced berries-yum!), go for the good stuff!

There is no love sincerer than the love of food.
- George Bernard Shaw

SNACK!

Boiled edamame.

A can of sardines.

Brown rice cake with almond butter and honey.

Peanut butter, banana, and honey on a slice of whole grain bread.

A serving of whole grain crackers (I love "Ak Mak") with 2 string cheeses.

12 almonds or walnuts and some 2% cottage cheese.

Carrots and a couple Tbsp. of hummus.

Natural (few added ingredients) turkey breast, spread with whole grain or honey mustard, wrapped around a string cheese.

Low fat or fat free plain yogurt (Greek is high in protein) and 12 nuts, with a little honey drizzle (add some fruit if you like!).

Scrambled egg whites and a slice of cheese.

Handful of soy nuts and an apple.

Small baked sweet potato (microwave comes in handy).

Low fat popcorn sprinkled with grated parmesan cheese.

Bowl of oatmeal with halved, raw walnuts, fresh blueberries, and a sprinkle of cinnamon.

¼ cup dry roasted pumpkin seeds and a pear.

An awesome treat of a sandwich: A small slice of whole grain bread spread with goat cheese, topped with a bit of chopped rosemary, about a Tbsp. of chopped walnuts, and a drizzle of honey.

Strawberries drizzled with a good balsamic vinegar and a scoop of 2 % cottage cheese on the side.

Greek yogurt with honey, a little chopped basil, and pistachios.

Jicama sticks (cut jicama as you would carrots, into "sticks") sprinkled with lime juice and a little salt—with some cayenne for a kick!

Tasty trail mix: roasted soybeans, dried cranberries, raw sunflower seeds, currants, raw cashew pieces, pumpkin seeds, sliced almonds, and unsweetened coconut chips.

Dining with one's friends and beloved family is certainly one of life's primal and most innocent delights, one that is both soul satisfying and eternal.
- Julia Child

SUGGESTED MENUS

Brunch:

To Your Health Crust-less Quiche

Quinoa Salad with Red Onions, Pecans, Goat Cheese, and Avocado

Golden Apricot Scones

Ginger Walnut Muffins with a Vanilla Cinnamon Glaze

Golden Pear Crisp

Dinner Parties with Friends:

I.

Warm Spinach Artichoke Dip

Grandma's Roasted Leg of Lamb

Best Caesar Salad

Chocolate Chip Bread Pudding

II.

Tomatoes with Bleu Cheese, Pine Nuts, and Basil

Flank Steak with a Bite

Baby Arugula Salad with Pecorino, Figs, and Pine Nuts

Dijon Roasted Cauliflower with Red Pepper and Walnuts

Chocolate Toffee Pecan Pie

Beginners:

I.

Whole Roasted Lemon Chicken- 7 Easy Steps

Reliable Rice

Broccolini with a Kick

In a Jiff Flourless Peanut Butter Cookies

II.

Speedy Choc-Full-Of-Good Turkey Chili

Spinach Salad with Blueberries, Strawberries, Walnuts, and Bleu Cheese

Ice Cream with Homemade Caramel Sauce and Bananas

Low Carb

I.

No Tortilla Chicken Enchiladas

Homemade Fresh Tomato Salsa

Go To Guacamole

Berries and Kiwi Fruit with Brown Sugar Vanilla Yogurt Sauce

II.

Crunchy Spiced Kale Chips

David's Asian Style Salmon

Sautéed Bok Choy with Sunflower Seeds

Homemade Cinnamon Applesauce

Practicing Cooks:

I.

Ultimate Deviled Eggs

Kale and Kidney Bean Soup

Old Fashioned Brisket

Balsamic Roasted Sweet Potatoes

Peach Blueberry Crumble

II.

Classic Hummus

Old World Tabeet

Raw Kale and Sweet Leaf Lettuce Salad

Fudge-y Flourless Chocolate Cake

Experienced Cooks:

I.

Toasted Parmesan Eggplant "Chips"

Pasta with Sundried Tomatoes and Goat Cheese

Parmesan Stuffed Mushrooms

Spinach, Roasted Beets, Mushrooms, and Sunflower Seed Salad with Citrus Vinaigrette

Chocolate Cupcakes with Shiny Chocolate Ganache

II.

Cannellini Bean Dip with Green Chiles and Figs

Butternut Squash Soup with Sage and Cranberries

Parmesan Crusted Tilapia

Pear Crouton, Gruyere, and Cashew Salad with Maple Champagne Vinaigrette

Baby Key Lime Pies with a Gingersnap Crust

RECIPE INDEX

Pizza Sauce (same page as Homemade Pizza with 5 Star Sauce) - p. 83

Potatoes:

Balsamic Roasted Sweet Potatoes - p. 144

Classic Latkes (Potato Pancakes) - p. 115

Roasted Potatoes (same page as Balsamic Roasted Sweet Potatoes) - p. 144

Whistler Mountain Roasted Carrots and Potatoes - p. 114

Quinoa:

Cinnamon Brown Sugar Quinoa Pudding with Toasted Almonds - p. 15

Quinoa Salad with Red Onions, Pecans, Goat Cheese, and Avocado - p. 60

Summer Quinoa Salad with Tomatoes, Fresh Basil, and Mozzarella - p. 74

Rice:

Jasmine Rice - p. 141

Mexican Rice - p. 141

Red Rice - p. 140

Reliable Rice - p. 140

Salad Dressings:

Bleu Cheese Vinaigrette - p. 77

Champagne Vinaigrette - p. 77

Citrus Vinaigrette - p. 77

Lemon and Olive Oil Dressing - p. 77

Red Wine Vinaigrette - p. 77

Sherry Vinaigrette - p. 77

Salads:

Baby Arugula, Fig, and Pecorino Salad with Pine Nuts - p. 64

Best Caesar Salad - p. 69

Colors Salad with Asian Honey-Lime Vinaigrette - p. 59

Lentil Salad with Indian Spiced Olive Oil-Lemon Vinaigrette - p. 67

Elli Samuels

Elli Samuels grew up in Highland Park, New Jersey, a quaint town about 45 minutes from New York City. She went to Rice University, where she met her husband of over 30 years, Tom. They have two children, whose college years and friendships were the inspiration for this book. Elli is a lawyer who went beyond, to her passion for cooking. She enjoys running, yoga, reading great books, looking at art and traveling. She splits her time between Houston, Texas and Hood River, Oregon.